The Complete Guide to the

FERRARI

308 · 328 · MONDIAL

The Complete Guide to the FERRARI 308 · 328 · MONDIAL

Wallace A. Wyss

DALTON WATSON

DALTON WATSON
The Arena Press/Dalton Watson plc
Russell Chambers
The Piazza
Covent Garden
LONDON
WC2E 8AA

First published as *The Complete Guide to the Ferrari 308 Series* 1982
First published in this revised edition 1988
Copyright © Wallace A. Wyss, 1982, 1988

British Library Cataloguing in Publication Data

Wyss, Wallace A.
 The complete guide to the Ferrari 308/328/Mondial
 rev. ed.
 1. Ferrari 308 & Mondial car – to 1987
 I. Title.
 629.2'222

 ISBN 0-901564-91-5

Printed by Scotprint Ltd, Musselburgh, Scotland

Contents

Acknowledgements

The author wishes to thank the following for their help and co-operation in the research of this book: Gary Bobileff; Serge Bellu (L'Automobile); Bertone S.p.A.; Winston S. Goodfellow; Robert E. Lee; Modena Sports Cars (Hollywood, Calif.); Motor-Presse International; Edwin K. Niles (Ferrari historian); Kurt Oblinger; Pininfarina S.p.A.; Quattroruote; Hilary Raab, Jr. (Ferrari historian); Wolfgang Rempath/Sportfahrer; Mike and Wilhelmina Sheehan (European Auto Restoration, Newport Beach, Calif.); Symbol; Lyle Tanner of LTE Enterprises; and Brian Winer. Special thanks are due to Andreoni Riccardo of Ferrari S.p.A., B.R.E. Turbochargers, Torrance, Calif. and Capt. Terry Phillips.

The 308 Spyder copied the lines of the coupe, except for the addition of "blind" rear 3/4 windows, covered by see-through louvers. The louvered panels are hinged to swing out once opened by key.

CHAPTER ONE

The Beginning

The farmer walks through the fields outside his vine-covered farmhouse. A sort of fog-like haze hangs over the Emilian plain, the weak sun of winter unable to burn it off.

The fog magnifies the sound of a car approaching at speed. The farmer looks up. It is a red car – low and powerful-looking. He listens to the engine note – the driver must still be in third, ah, there, he has upshifted to fourth. The sound is menacing and guttural, not a twelve certainly, but very possibly a V8.

The car is closer now, drifting around the curve before the farmer's entrance road. The farmer can see the familiar yellow rectangle and prancing horse insignia on the chest of the test driver's coveralls. The test driver nods and the farmer waves back, suddenly remembering Taruffi, Ascari, De Portago and the others. If only they could see him now – a racer who is now a farmer!

A moment later, the car is gone, and the farmer hears only a high-pitched whine hanging in the air as the driver upshifts at 7700 rpm to fifth. . . .

In the rest of the world – save the United States – the Ferrari flagship is the potent 12-cylinder mid-engined "Boxer", a car that is now over 10 years in production but which, like the shark, seems to have the ability to survive all challenges in its element.

In the United States – beset by a tangle of emissions and safety laws – the Ferrari crest is carried only by the 308, a series of mid-engined cars descended from the Boxer design, and powered by a 4-cam V8 that continues in the long tradition of high-revving vee-type engines from the world's most famous name in racing.

Ferrari is not the only firm making mid-engined V8-powered cars in Italy. Lamborghini makes the Jalpa and DeTomaso still flogs the ageing – but up-dated Pantera, now 12 years in production.

But the 308 GT4 enjoys the luxury of being produced by a firm that has the resources to produce it in sufficient quantity and to distribute it world-wide. Cars roll out of the Ferrari factory by the *hour*, where DeTomaso and Lamborghini manage only a couple of cars per *week*.

Prova Mo

The chassis for all Ferrari production cars are made outside – by a supplier, in the same way that DeTomaso, Maserati and others buy the basic framework from firms that specialize only in making the tube or unitized chassis.

The chassis is then fitted with a floor pan and inner fenderwells, and a unitized body fabricated by Ferrari fitted over the tube frame. This is what makes a Ferrari 308 so strong – it is essentially a unitized body built *atop* a tubular frame, reflecting a cautious belt-plus-suspenders approach.

The car then is painted, inside and out; wired, upholstered, fitted with a suspension, wheels, tires and instrumentation.

Meanwhile the engine has been assembled and run for eight hours on a test bench. Only firms like Aston Martin, Rolls-Royce, Bentley, Lamborghini and Bristol do this kind of pre-installation testing.

Except for the painting, the rest of the assembly takes only a few hours. Then Ferrari again departs from the procedures used by manufacturers of "mass-produced" cars – they take the brand-new car out and drive it at least 100 km on a pre-planned route around the town of Maranello. Come rain, or shine, snow or hail, the brand new Ferraris, wearing temporary "PROVA MO" (test car, Modena) plates, roll out of the factory door every few minutes, their exhausts rapping as they rocket down the two-lane roads.

The ultimate "collectable" in terms of a Ferraristi might be the wooden body buck used as a "former" for the first metal parts. These life-size bucks are used to guide the development of the initial metal parts. Then, as shown in this 1978 photo, they are simply and unceremoniously thrown away! (Hilary A Raab Jnr.)

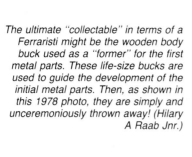

Yes, Ferrari still uses tubular frames somewhat like the old A.C. Cobra. No, Ferrari doesn't make them. They're delivered from outside. Here's a stack of European & Australian 308 chassis. Some read "AB 553" written in chalk. This means"308GTB". (Hilary A. Raab Jnr.)

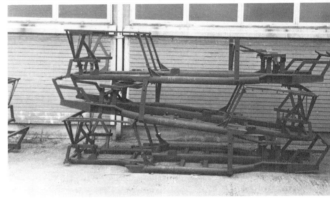

You have to be a chassis expert to spot this but this American-spec chassis have extra bracing for the bumper mounts and between the engine and cockpit. Chalk markings on these frames say "USA". (Hilary A. Raab Jnr.)

A scene shot in the Ferrari works at Maranello in May, 1982, shows a half-dozen GTS models and a couple of Mondial 8's still sitting on the hand-pushed trolleys prior to being put on the assembly line where the interior, electrics, instrumentation and upholstery would be installed.

Foam sheets cover the paintwork as the car goes down the assembly line.

Coil-over-shock rear suspension assemblies sit on a bench at the Ferrari factory in Maranello.

The machining of the 308 engine is done to the same high standard as the V12's. Although the bores look so close together that one might conclude there is no room for increased displacement, some speculate that 4 liters out of that block is not impossible. (Hilary A. Raab Jnr.)

Ferrari casts its own engine blocks and machines and assembles them all in one building. Their attention to machining and balancing is perhaps the best among the world's exotic car makers.

The wiring for Ferraris grows more complicated as the demand grows by consumers for more luxuries. This is a Mondial 8 interior about two hours away from being completed and road tested.

The emissions test is an important part of making certain a Ferrari is "right" before it leaves Maranello.

These cars have just finished their road test and are going to be evaluated mechanically with reference to the driver's "score sheet."

When each car returns, it is checked out on the dyno to evaluate any faults noticed by the test driver and re-tuned. The car is then cleaned, any paint flaws corrected, and then sent to the final detailing room, a room so clean it looks like a surgeon's amphitheatre. There the cars are detailed so well that the only clue each has *ever* been driven is the numbers clicked up on the odometer. The final step is preparation for shipment to any one of over 260 Ferrari dealers in almost thirty different countries.

There is a certain philosophy in the building of a Ferrari that explains in large part the devotional attitude of enthusiasts for the marque. Ferrari still does a few things almost unique among auto-makers. It still casts its own engines where many auto-makers prefer to have these made elsewhere by private suppliers. The same goes for the gearboxes – Ferrari making their own where even Aston Martin uses ZF's from Germany or Turbo-Hydra-matics from the U.S.

Ferrari is also a nationalistic concern, its car being composed of about 95% "local content", with only its fuel injection (German-made), catalytic converter (American-made) and turbocharger (German-made) coming from other countries, unless you want to count the leather, which comes from Connolly in England but which is still cut and stitched together in Maranello. In "local content", Ferrari runs neck-and-neck with Lotus, who pride themselves on being largely an English car, except for the German-made wheels and French-made transaxle on the Turbo Esprit.

Ferrari's test drive for each and every car would be labeled anachronistic and time-consuming by most of the world's auto-makers and, admittedly, this same practice gives American customers a moment of pause, for they are used to buying a new car with, say, 7 miles on the clock, not 70. It makes one wonder – after looking at the break-in recommendations in the Owner's Manual – if the test driver *really* kept the revs below 4500 rpm in his sprint across the Emilian plain.

On the other hand, other auto-makers – save Porsche – would be jealous of Ferrari's Fiorano test track which is one of the most well-instrumented in the world. Essentially, it was originally set up to monitor subtle changes in Grand Prix car performance. Since it was designed to handle cars going well over 300 kph, accurately clocking a 200-plus kph car like the 308 is much easier. With its closed-circuit TV and telemetry systems (sending readings to computers), the Fiorano track can be used to gauge whether any particular engine/suspension configuration is "right" for a Ferrari.

The Fiorano track, built in 1972, with several Ferrari sponsors sharing the costs, including Firestone, Shell, Marelli (who supplied the electronic TV-scanners used for remote control incident detecting) and Heuer (who provided an electronic timing system). It is 3 Km (1.86 miles) long and 27.5 feet wide. It has 14 corners, about evenly distributed between right and left-hand turns, and, unlike most real race-tracks, has little in the way of Armco barriers. Ferrari doesn't need them – there being no spectators, but there is one netting at the sharpest hairpin to stop a Ferrari driver from ending up out on a busy Modena street.

It is a figure-eight in layout, using a bridge for the cross-over point.

Because the track occupies such a limited area, it wasn't possible to design for the maximum speed of a GP car, so the fastest attainable speed on the straight is just short of 170-mph – or just enough to get a 512 Boxer up to speed.

The way the track works is this: as the car shoots past the timing building, it trips off the first photocell and the timing of the lap begins. A computer printout shows the time elapsed between each successive photocell as well as records the overall time. Thus, it can be seen how fast different drivers took the same corner; who is better at braking and so forth. Since Turn 4 is a constant radius, cornering force can also be measured, and it is interesting that a T5 Grand Prix car recorded a 2.2 lateral *g*-force reading back in 1980, while a 308GTB on XWX Michelin's usually records .87 when pushed to the limit.

"The Only Real Ferrari . . ."

Enzo Ferrari reportedly once told a reporter "A real Ferrari has 12 cylinders", a remark which he no doubt regretted for decades afterward. In truth, one has only to make the most cursory study of Ferrari racing history to find four-cylinder, six-cylinder and eight-cylinder cars which dominated their classes as well as the twelves. Although Enzo Ferrari made the V12 his own personal obsession from 1947 onwards, there was no less care shown in the design of other Ferrari engines.

Those elitists who denigrate the 308 by saying "That is not a Ferrari, but a Fiat", ignore what you can see on a factory tour: the Boxers, 400's and 308's are all coming off the same assembly lines. The engine blocks are all cast in the same place, they are all assembled by the same mechanics, they are all driven by the same test drivers over all the same routes or on the same test track.

No, the 308, despite what the owners of V12 Ferraris like to say, is not in any way, shape or form to be construed a "badge-engineered special" like the Daimler Double Six, which is merely a Jaguar with a different grille, or, worse yet, the Porsche 924 which was *built* by Audi, *powered* by VW, but *sold* under the name Porsche.

The only basis an elitist would have firm ground to stand on in establishing a pecking order with 308's is by stressing the truly enviable difference between European and American-specification versions – the European versions being 200 lbs. lighter, with 30 more horsepower and a 10-mph higher top speed. But it's no use for American customers to lament – the same enforced differentiation exists between the American and European specification versions of *many* imports, from the Porsche 928 to the Jaguar XJ-S. The Europeans get the fast versions while the Americans get the slow ones, *but* the Americans have the advantage of being able to buy petrol at roughly 1/3rd to 1/4th the European price. You pick your country and you take your choice. . . .

Fiat first bought into SEFAC Ferrari in the late '60's, by originally pumping infusions of *lira*, finally ending up by owning it lock, stock and barrel along with Lancia, Autobianchi and Abarth, other marques they had absorbed earlier. But it is remarkable how little they have affected it other than to improve it – to keep its standards relevant in a changing world.

There are those who lament "the day the Old Man sold out" or the day of the Fiat-Ferrari marriage. But when one considers the alternatives – such as marriage to an American firm (Ford courted Enzo Ferrari for two weeks in 1963, only to have the Commendatore abruptly cancel negotiations) or a complete dropping of the racing program (such as Maserati did in the early 60's), then the merger seems the best compromise.

It allowed Ferrari to continue to race competitively in Formula 1, the word "competitive" translating to "sufficient financial resources to outspend the competition", and when one considers that at least one team from 1980 has been supported by Saudi-Arabian oil money, one can see that remaining competitive with such a team involves heavy expenditures.

Ferrari's Formula 1 racing activities have what a Detroit ad executive would call "good rub-off," for there's always the implied existence of a "trickle-down" situation where "What's learned on the track today can be used on the street cars tomorrow." Ferrari and Lotus both increasingly tie in their Formula 1 activities with their street cars, and the 1982 introductory 208 Turbo brochure had a picture of works driver Didier Pironi with a 208 Turbo. (Lamborghini refutes the value of a racing team entirely by continuing to sell rivals to the Boxer, and their factory has never run a racing team – ever.)

But one nagging thought about racing is that it saps up a lot of Ferrari's engineering talent; talent that might well be devoted to solving problems, say, in the U.S.-specification 308's. One gets the impression when visiting Ferrari that the U.S. models are not very important to them compared to their racing program, and their European models, yet the U.S. market accounts for over 50% of their sales!

CHAPTER TWO

The GT4

It was low, and squat. They could tell that much as it pulled into the Shell station for benzina. The test driver jumped out and began to direct the pumping of fuel into the car, his eyes shifting nervously – always on the lookout for "spy" photographers with their long-distance lenses.

The gas station employees circled the car. The four exhaust pipes were no clue to the number of cylinders. The Bertone crest was significant – Bertone being active in the development of Lamborghini's mid-engined cars.

The fuel tank topped off, the driver belted himself in again, and pulled on his driving gloves. There was the WHIRR of an electric fuel pump and the exhaust pipes erupted with noise, a harsh guttural bark.

The driver pulled it into first, eased out to the edge of the street, looked for an opening and floored it. At high rpm, the sound took on an unmistakable note: Ferrari. One attendant looked at the other and shrugged. "It was beautiful," he said. "but it doesn't look like a Ferrari."

308 GT4

The choice of Carrozzeria Bertone for the design was not only what set the new 308 apart from other Ferraris but also what perhaps doomed the car from the start. The 308 GT4 made its debut in October, 1973 at the Paris Salon, where it surprised everyone by being such a radical departure from the styles set by Ferrari's usual body designer, Pininfarina.

Gone were the traditional sensuous humps over the wheelwells, gone were the traditional circular taillamps, gone were the expected in-the-flanks engine air intakes, or the reverse wrap-around rear window. In short, all that had comprised the Pininfarina-designed 206/246 Dino was thrown out; scrapped. In the GT4, Bertone was introducing Ferrari to "The Wedge Look", but, in doing so, selling them a design that could just as well have been intended for one of the Lamborghini Urraco series, which Carrozzeria Bertone also designed.

Not that the 308 GT4 was a bad design in and of itself. GM designer Gerry Palmer, an avid Ferrari enthusiast, feels that "it is the more unexpected design, braver than the 308 GTB that followed". And, indeed, the 308 GT4, while lacking the sensuality of Pininfarina Ferraris, does have many little-recognized virtues of its own – subtle things like the almost flush air intakes behind the side windows, and the flat tail-lamps which aesthetically and aerodynamically fit the flat tail much better than do the traditional round ones on the Pininfarina-designed Ferraris.

It is perhaps unfair to compare the 308 with the 246 Dino. True, both are Dinos, both are mid-engined Ferraris, and one followed the other chronologically. But the 308 GT4 was not really intended to replace the 246 Dino coupe and spyder. That would come later. Rather it was intended to be the first of a whole *new* class of Ferrari sports cars.

The 246 Dino had a few flaws, to be sure: its cam-drive chains stretched unless they were periodically tightened, its air conditioning, in the words of one owner, "didn't work even when it worked", but it wasn't those flaws that killed the series. It was simply that Ferrari couldn't use its V6 engine for more than that configuration – it wouldn't have had the torque to power a 2-plus-2, for instance.

Another reason the 246 Dino was phased out was simply because tastes in the automotive design world had changed – mostly as a result of Giorgetto Giugiaro's pushing of "The Wedge" shape, most exemplified by his Lotus Esprit design. Ferrari selected Bertone in order to move away from the curve. The later Pininfarina-designed 308 GTB/GTS/Mondial 8 were moves back toward a combination of the flat and curved-surface trends, and, ironically, after starting the whole automotive world on "The Wedge", Giugiaro has switched back to curves again.

Perhaps because it is no longer with us, the 246 Dino – at least in its open-top GTS form – is already a hot collector's classic and worth enough to justify the expense of ground-up restorations. Having had a ride in one courtesy of a Ferrari Owner's Club member around Riverside Raceway at speed, this writer can testify that it had a lightness, a zinginess that is missing in the U.S. version of the 308 GTB/GTS. After all, the car weighs 780 lbs. less than its successor and is unencumbered with a catalytic converter or "safety bumpers." It can be shifted, and drifted through the esses, with an astonishing alacrity, and driven to the limit with utter predictability.

When it became apparent that there was a need for a new generation, a V8 replacement was planned. Why a V8? Perhaps it isn't appreciated by Americans – who are used to V8's and take them for granted – that the V8 remains one of the most balanced reciprocating-piston engine configurations, the pulses cancelling each other out so that it has less inherent vibration than a V6 and far less than an in-line four or V4. More power, more torque and more smoothness was what Ferrari was after.

The Type F106A engine was traditional Ferrari in most respects – aluminum block (Ferrari calls it by its trade name Siluminum), aluminum hemispherical heads, inclined overhead valves with four overhead camshafts and thimble-type tappets, five main bearings (instead of the seven as used in the V12), shrunk in cast-iron cylinder liners, Marelli distributors and a quartet of Weber updraft two-barrel carburetors.

Where the new engine differed from previous Ferrari *production* cars was in its V8 configuration (previous Ferrari V8's being used only in racing) and in the use of cogged (toothed) rubber belts located outside the engine to drive the cam rather than chains. Actually, these belts had been used on the

Ferrari flat-12 powering the 365 Boxer, but this was the first Ferrari vee-type engine to use them. Ferrari said they were less prone to breakage or stretching than chains lasting at least 15,000 miles before they need changing. (Though some Ferrari mechanics point out that chains often last 50,000 miles before they need changing!) True, one of the great sounds – chains clanking and rattling – is lost in the Ferrari "symphony" but then it is hopeless to think a thundering V8 can come close to matching the shriek of V12 anyway.

The GT4 was also wet-sump, another "downgrade" in the eyes of the cognoscenti from the V12 cars, but the truth is that many dry-sump cars run so cool in traffic that the oil never even gets *warm*. Not that many street Ferraris were wet-sump anyway, just enough to make this feature seem exotic.

The actual horsepower rating is a bone of contention. Originally, Ferrari rated the V8 at 255 bhp at 7700 rpm in Italy. The U.S. smogified versions – with an 8.8:1 compression ratio, Weber 40 DCN carburetors, plus an air pump – produced 205 bhp at 6600 rpm. *Motor* magazine, in their March, 1976 test, quotes a figure of 250 bhp (DIN) at 7700 rpm for a British model with 40 DCNF carburetors and an 8.8:1 compression ratio.

Even though different magazine road testers quoted different horsepower figures for the engine, the highest "official" quote was 255 bhp, and generally it can be said that: "the earlier the engine, the more power it put out," simply because the U.S. version of the 308 became more and more encumbered with smog controls as time went on. The European models are good for at least 30 more horsepower than the American-specification models *if* they are fitted with the European exhausts. Another general rule is that carburetored 308 engines are more powerful than fuel-injected ones, but this comment should be qualified by the fact that, at this writing, no magazine road tester has yet reported on the performance of the 1982½ 4-valve fuel-injected Mondial in European-specification trim. Ferrari started out with a potent engine for the 308 in 1974 and let it go soft. As of late 1982, there were signs they finally recognized this and were intent on reviving more power from the Type F106A block.

Front 3/4 view of the clay model shows much more pronounced front hood vents were considered. Side air intake scoops were segmented in this early proposal too.

308GTB-type rear deck lid vents were originally planned for ventilation. This is the clay model at Bertone. Note slots in roof rear edge.

A Word About The Name "Dino" . . .

The "Dino" name entered Ferrari genealogy by virtue of the fact that "Dino" was the nickname of Enzo Ferrari's son, Alfredo, who died at the age of 25 of leukemia. Prior to his death, Dino was active in engine design for Formula 2, and had in fact developed a V6 which was used in a Ferrari Formula 2 design (It even had the name "Dino" molded into the valve covers).

Since this engine was the basis for the Dino V6 used in the Fiat Dino production car (with engine built by Fiat, under license from Ferrari) and later the 206/246 mid-engined Ferraris, those cars were called "Dinos", and wore appropriate insignia consisting of a stylized signature of the name "Dino", usually depicted in blue lettering on a yellow background.

Many people assume that the 308's V8 was but the old 246 Dino upscaled in cylinders and displacement but it is actually more like a Daytona engine with four cylinders lopped off, as is evident by the fact that the Daytona pistons fit the 308, which has the same bore and stroke. The 308 engine is tuned to the same level as well, putting out 85 hp. per liter, while the Daytona — if you accept "352 hp" as the stock output-put out 80 hp. per liter.

But 1974 — the year of the new Dino's introduction — was also the year of the Arab oil embargo and exotic car sales bottomed out just as the economies in all the oil-using countries did. Ferrari dealers in the U.S. began to feel that it was already hard enough to sell the Bertone wedge-design 308 in a sick economy without always having to explain "Well, yes it's a *Ferrari* but it's called Dino because, etc. etc.".

Ferrari's first move to solve this problem was in 1976 when they began attaching the prancing horse insignia to the rear valance panels. Their second concession — first seen in Pininfarina's GTB design — was to put the word "Ferrari" or the prancing horse emblem on the car, not just once but many times Ferrari appeared schizoid about this — sometimes GT4's shown in the same brochure would be wearing "Dino" center emblems on the wheels in one picture and prancing horse insignia in the next. By 1980, the use of the prancing horse insignia had reached almost ridiculous proportions — one *Car and Driver* editor finding either the word "Ferrari" or the prancing horse insignia on his test GTB no less than 11 times.

According to Hilary Raab Jr., an acknowledged Ferrari historian, the early Pininfarina-built GTB prototypes wore "Dino" insignia rather than Ferrari crests, leading one to conclude that — at Pininfarina — they conceived of the GTB as a successor to the 246 series rather than as a *Ferrari* per se. Evidently when Bertone was forced to switch to Ferrari regalia, Pininfarina was able to make the switch on their prototype before their design "hardened" into a final design.

The 308 GTB "Dino" was a car of confused identities. While at first the plaque "Dino" went on the cars, pressure from American Ferrari dealers later forced Ferrari to include the prancing horse and downplay the name "Dino."

The V8 engine was placed sideways (transversely) in the chassis as was the V6 in the 206/246 Dino, as opposed to the *other* way of building a mid-engine car, which is to set the engine longitudinally (length-wise) which, in this writer's mind, and, as seen in the Pantera, makes it far easier to work on. Before one asserts that the transverse location makes for ideal weight distribution, the European GT4's weight distribution was 43% front/57% rear, hardly close to the generally-considered "ideal" of 50/50. (But then that 50/50 figure came from front-engined rear wheel drive cars. The "ideal" for mid-engined cars is more like 40% front 60% rear). Possibly, the transverse configuration might have been chosen solely as a means of providing trunk room behind the engine but one should be warned that it costs much more to service the engine *because* it is transverse because of the increased difficulty of reaching the spark plugs on the far side of the engine. It is interesting to note that the very first mid-engined Dino prototype of 1965 had a longitudinally-mounted V6, a configuration shared by all of Ferrari's successful V-12-powered mid-engined racing cars like the 250LM, P3 and P4. But then, *they* didn't have to carry any luggage. (Unless you want to count the FIA-suitcase which was a joke anyway!)

The very first mid-engined non-racing Dino was this 1965 prototype with quad headlamps under glass, knock-off wheels, a full hatchback and a longitudinally-mounted V6. It had non-circular taillamps—out of character for Ferrar—and rear louvers for venting hot air out of the engine compartment. It is thought that the roof on this model was deliberately set low, so that it looked more dramatic than it would have been if set at a practical height. That's a legitimate trick for show cars.

To avoid excessive height of the engine and transmission combination, the gearbox is set behind the engine. It actually shares the engine sump case similar to the Lamborghini Miura and Miura S but, as in the Miura SV, separates the two oils needed to lubricate each.

The all-synchromesh gearbox is made by Ferrari and uses helical spur-type gears and a limited slip differential. The drive shafts are solid with constant velocity joints (sliding types on the inside) to allow for suspension movement. The synchromesh design is from Porsche though Porsche ones are *not* interchangeable.

The suspension consisted of upper and lower wishbones and coil springs all the way around, using telescopic Koni shock absorbers. An anti-roll bar, is used both front and rear. Earlier 308 GT4's came with six-spoke Cromodora light-alloy wheels, sized 6.5" × 14", but the late 1977 through 1979 U.S. models came with Campagnolo six-spoke, or Campagnolo or Speedline five-spoke Daytona-style "star" mags, the latter preferred by Americans because they gave the car more of a "pure" Ferrari look since the early GT4 wheels had also been standard on the Fiat Dino (a nice car which had the curse of being named "Fiat" although it had a Ferrari engine).

The initial choice in tires was Michelin XWX steel-braced tubeless radials, sized 205/70VR-14. One choice facing every manufacturer of a mid-engined sports car is: "Should the rear tires be made wider than the fronts?" The reason this question is asked is because, again, there is always that lurking possibility of trailing throttle oversteer, where an injudicious cornering manuver can result in a spinout. The way to counteract this tendency is to put more rubber on the road in the rear so that the rear end will have more resistance to coming unstuck. The Pantera has always had two different sized wheels and tires, and the Lamborghini Countach S remains the most obvious example of this. Ferrari's Boxer, after first trying same-size wheels and tires all the way around on the 365, finally switched to wider wheels and tires on the rear of the 512.

But on the 308 series, Ferrari has so far refused to resort to this alternative, perhaps because the 308's, collectively, are viewed as more practical *road* cars than the Boxers are. The problem with having different-sized wheels and tires does not occur until you have a flat. Since you can only carry one spare, running different sizes front and rear makes for a 50% chance of the spare being the wrong size when you need it. By having *all* the wheels and tires the same size, this problem is eliminated.

The early GT4's had the Cromodora mag wheels with tiny hubcaps covering the lug nuts. This picture is dated "Ottobre 73," indicating prototypes were already finished well before the car made its debut as a 1974 model.

The wider-tires-on-the-back philosophy is also recognized by many as only a "band-aid" solution. A better solution is to design the car to be a basic understeerer, one that won't go into oversteer even if the driver is so dim-witted as to brake or lift off the throttle in the middle of a curve (and sometimes it can't be helped!). The 308's, collectively, are like that. Some models are more "tail-happy" than others but none even comes close to having lethal handling characteristics like the DeTomaso Mangusta or Monteverdi Hai, both of which had much heavier cast-iron Detroit-built V8's mounted longitudinally amidships.

The brakes were ventilated discs all around with servo assist being standard and a pressure regulator used at the rear of the split circuits to keep the action even. *Motor* magazine's road testers, in a March, 1976 test, said the brakes "proved well up to the task with an ability to claw the car down from high speeds repeatedly", but they found quite a bit of pressure – 80 lbs. – was needed to effect the optimum stop, at 0.95 *g*. The car might have gone to 1 *g* but was limited by front wheel locking.

Road Test was the only U.S. magazine to really criticise the GT4 brakes. "Although perfectly acceptable", they wrote, "164 feet from 60 mph is hardly world-shattering braking, and in a panic stop, the front wheels would alternately lock up, causing us to slow down in a lurching left-right dance. And *that* really surprised us, because on the road the brakes felt powerful and well-balanced; perhaps the difference between carefully-modulated racing stops and panic stops hasn't been programmed into the Ferrari computer. Expert drivers try to avoid the all-wheels-locked condition at all costs, but most drivers simply stab the brake pedal in an emergency".

The dashboard layout was reminiscent of the 246 in that all the gauges were grouped in a cluster in a hooded nacelle, though this nacelle was stretched out about 1/3rd wider than in the 246 Dino to include toggles and slide levers as well as gauges. The two large-diameter gauges were the 10,000-rpm tachometer and the 180 mph speedometer. Outside these were the gauges for fuel, and engine oil temperature. Between the two big dials were smaller dials indicating water temperature and oil pressure and a clock. A bit busy, to be sure, and *Motor's* road testers found that – if one drove with one's hands in the recommended 10 o'clock-2 o'clock driving position "the top sections of the rev counter and speedometer are out of sight". The instrument panel thrust outwards toward the driver at each end – the right side having the heater controls and the left the traditional toggle switches for the emergency flasher, fog lamps and blower motor.

Topping off the instruments was the Momo steering wheel which had aluminum spokes, a leather-covered rim and a blue-on yellow styleized "Dino" signature. Since they had run out of room on the instrument panel, there was an additional mini-console to the back of the shifter with everything else grouped together in a rather bewildering array, including the electric window buttons, rear window defroster switch, cigarette lighter, choke and the radio, the latter mounted longitudinally almost as an afterthought, even in line with the driver's hip.

The 308 GT4 dashboard was sensibly laid out—with a big tachometer on the right, a speedometer on the left and oil pressure and water temperature needles and a clock squeezed between the two. In this European model, the gauges still read "Dino" while the steering wheel has a Ferrari prancing horse, symbolizing the confusion in product identification Ferrari had at this time.

While in the days of the V12 Ferrari drivers often drove listening only to the music of the engine, anyone driving a 308 Dino took his life in his hands if he tried to tune into a radio station with his eye on the dial.

Once upon a time, Ferraris – the Daytona coming first to mind – had this non-glare covering – a sort of no-fluff velour finish – on the tops of the dashboard. While it looked tacky and gathered lint like a magnet, this material also effectively prevented the sun's glare from bothering the driver. Well, when Bertone designed the GT4, (it was built by Scaglietti) they decided that the fast-fading velour should be replaced by nice shiny vinyl. The result? The glare came back. In bright sunlight, it's particularly annoying. (Somehow, today's designers ought to be sentenced to driving some 60's supercars so they would know *why*

things were done the way they were . . .) Yet another problem with vinyl is that it and the glue its stuck on with, generates a film on the inside of the windscreen. It can easily be wiped off, but it's a nuisance.

Ferraris don't come with many options, and even what's optional varies from country to country. The GT4's came into England with electric windows, a rear screen defroster and tinted windows – all "standard" already mounted extras for which you were charged nearly £200. It was possible to order a car especially without these, however. Other options in England were air conditioning (£374), metallic paint (£152), leather seats instead of cloth (£301.86), an electric sunroof (£265) and 1" wider wheels (£222). A "fully-loaded" GT4, then cost £12,500 compared to the "stripped" price of a mere £11,000.

In Europe, the GT4 came standard with cloth upholstery with leather bolsters. The cloth could be counted on to show signs of fade and wear sooner than the leather.

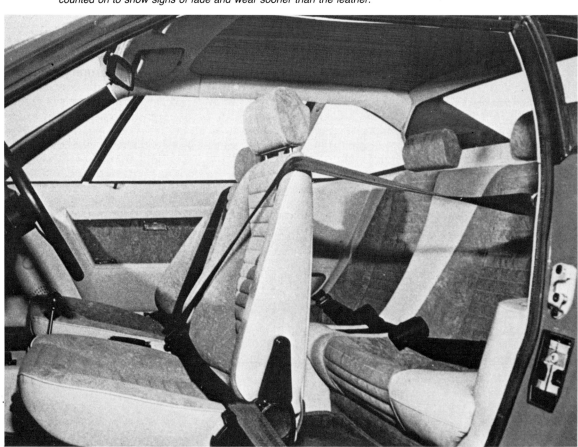

Although the 308 GT4 was called a "2-plus-2" in Europe and sold as a 4-seater, apparently a few were delivered with only carpeting in the back and aluminum screwed-in "rub rails" for luggage to rest on – 3 rails on the carpeted floor and three on the carpeted firewall. In addition, cars so fitted out had two lengthy belt-like straps for securing luggage in place. This layout made the 308 GT4 much more practical for long trips, especially if the owner had no children and liked to enjoy his fast driving with only one companion.

The GT4 not only had the release levers for the engine cover lid and boot (luggage compartment) lid hidden by the door itself, but the levers themselves were lockable so even if a thief got your door open, he couldn't unlock the levers. The Bertone 308 also had a glovebox but once you folded down the lid, most of the space was filled with fuses. (This is still better than the Pininfarina-designed 308 GTS which has only door pockets and no glovebox).

One of the areas where the Bertone GT4 most disturbed Ferrari "purists" was that it marked the return to quadruple headlamps (like the poor 330 GT 2-plus-2 of the early 60's). By moving two control stalks one could turn on first the side marker lamps and then the main beams. Daylight flashing (to signal when over-taking) with the headlights down was accomplished by pulling the stalk toward the steering wheel to blink the road lamps, if it had them (most European specification cars did).

The 308 GT4 was considered a four-seater, on paper, but as Motor's road testers wrote in 1976: "front and rear seat passengers must compromise considerably if all are to travel in any comfort". They did, however, use the car as a four-seater for short journeys, proving to themselves it was possible just as one occasionally sees four in a Porsche 911.

Performance

Ferrari wanted three things out of the 308 V8 that they didn't have in the 246:
1.) Torque
2.) Smoothness
3.) Potential
They got the first two easily, by the increase in displacement first of all and by the inherent balance of a V8 as opposed to a V6. The full potential of the engine is still to be fully realized at this writing. Even with the "siamesed" look of the bores, there is still room to make the bores bigger and a four-liter version is not impossible. The decision to go larger than 3 liters is more a political one than one of whether or not it can be done.

The performance of the 308 GT4 varied according to specifications and to which country it was imported. The European-spec models had the advantage of much lighter, smaller bumpers and the absence of an energy-robbing smog pump or thermal reactor. Motor magazine's road testers hold the record for squeezing the highest top speed from one. They managed a high of 154 mph (248 kph) using a 7300 rpm redline. Their speed, in fact, was higher than they achieved with three previous 4-seater sports cars – the Porsche Carrera 3 (Sportomatic), Jaguar XJ-S or Urraco P250. (How things have changed – by 1982, the vastly-improved Jaguar XJ-S HE beats the Ferrari Mondial 8 by 10 mph).

Motor also achieved a 0–60 mph time of 6.9 seconds – a good "supercar" time compared to the average of 7 seconds for late 60's American supercars like the 427 Corvette. Road & Track, in America, printed a test written by Paul Frère, their European correspondent, in September, 1974. Frère, a former race driver and Le Mans competitor, got a 0 to 60 mph time of 6.4 seconds and a top speed of 152 mph from a European version using only a 6700 rpm redline but when Road & Track tested a U.S. version later, they were only able to turn a 0 to 60 mph time of 8 seconds and reach a top speed of only 138 mph.

Paul Frère described the engine of the GT4 thus: "There isn't the slightest problem in driving the Dino in heavy town traffic, and it makes life so easy on motorways where, after having had to slow down to 80–90 mph, all you have to do is stay in 5th gear and push your right foot down to zoom past the car that got in your way. In fact the engine will accelerate in 5th gear from 1000–1100 rpm (25 mph) and soar right up to its maximum speed of 152 mph without flat spots or cam effects being felt".

More proof that the European GT4's were hot performers was provided in late 1974 by Germany's *Auto Motor und Sport*, whose GT4 test car proved to be faster overall than the DeTomaso Pantera, Maserati Merak and Porsche Carrera they had previously tested. The reported speeds were:

	308 GT4	Pantera	Merak	Porsche C Carrera
0–100 Km/h	6.8 sec.	6.6 sec.	9.3 sec.	6.1 sec.
Standing start 1 Km	26.7 sec.	26.9 sec.	30.1 sec.	26.2 sec
Top Speed	248.3 Km/h	244.9 Km/h	235.3 Km/h	238.4 Km/h

The U.S. version of the GT4 had a monumental front bumper similar in size and shape to a railroad tie. Gone were the road lamps of the European versions, as well as the circular front fender side marker lamps.

Because of the ultra-short bumper on European models, the grille cavity was a lot more evident than on American versions. This one has Carello lamps fitted as standard equipment.

They quoted their car as having a 236 hp rating at 6600 rpm, which translated to 80.7 hp. per liter. Torque was 28 mkg at 5000 rpm. Their car weighed 1320 Kg. quite a bit less than the U.S. version. Yet another reason European-market cars may prove faster than U.S.-spec versions is that they have higher, thus more potent, octane gas there instead of the low octane "junk gas" sold in the U.S. When the GT4 was reviewed from a collector's standpoint in the June 1982 *Thoroughbred & Classic Car*, they wrote: "Vigour you expect but what impressed us even more about this engine – by far the best part of the drivetrain, in fact the best feature of the car – was how smooth, healthy and mechanically fit it still felt and sounded. Make no mistake, Ferrari's 3-liter V8 gem ranks among the greats". But enthusiasm didn't extend to the clutch: "Those flaws," they said, "which to some degree marred the transmission were for the most part inherent, not inflicted by wear and tear. The clutch is not only very heavy but irksomely long in travel, though the fluid smoothness of its engagement is a strong redeeming feature in stop-start traffic, particularly as the engine is so smooth and tractable at the bottom end. Snatch in the drivetrain at low speeds in fourth or fifth deters high-gear pottering, though."

In their road test, *Road & Track* reported: "Shift gears at the 7700-rpm redline and more often than not the lever slides into the proper gate but the transmission remains in neutral. To avoid this we lowered our shift points to 7000 rpm. So a properly performing Dino would be quicker still". Thus, one can see how a single improperly-prepared test car can doom an exotic car to a "slow" image when just one major magazine road tests it.

Road Test magazine was the only U.S. magazine to really criticize the clutch design: "(the) clutch failed to engage more often than not when making shifts at high engine speeds, (causing) the tach (to go) over the 7700 rpm final redline. The reason was traceable and to us puzzling. The Ferrari Dino is equipped with a diaphragm clutch, and the hot rodders in this country have known about diaphragm clutches for years.

"A diaphragm clutch is almost standard fare for most domestic cars because it requires relatively little pedal effort in comparison to a coil-spring unit. But diaphragm clutches have a serious drawback for high-speed applications. In action they are a Belleville spring, or a flat circular piece of metal which, when activated, is deformed into a shallow cone.

"At high speeds the fingers, the parts of the spring which contact the throwout bearing, go over center and centrifugal force holds them there with a resultant failure of the clutch to re-engage. The pedal simply stays on the floor until the revs come back down. To us, with a car that costs $25,000 and [has] a screamer of an engine, plus the world's number one image of blasting performance, this clutch is inexcusable".

A more oft-heard complaint is the heaviness of the clutch. *Road & Track*, in a July, 1978 road test, asked: "does the clutch effort have to be so heavy? The stiffness isn't particularly noticeable when you're driving hard, but around-town motoring provides more exercise for a driver's leg than a Charles Atlas weight-lifting course".

The noise the 308 made wasn't always loved. *Road Test*, in their March 1976 test, wrote: "the noise level is something only an enthusiast could tolerate and only a Ferrari freak could love. At 70 mph our noise meter shook around the 81 dBA mark, and at full throttle in first gear it reached 93. Now, to approximate the quality of the noise, harken back to the soundtrack of *"Bullitt"* and conjure the noise McQueen's Mustang made in full flight. Double *that* and you have the sound of a twincam* Ferrari V8 running flat out behind your right ear. After two hours of driving, we didn't *need* the radio; we couldn't have heard it anyway".

Road & Track's staffers, in a 1975 comparison test between the GT4, the Urraco P111 and the Merak, said: "(The Dino V8) has a sound unlike any American V8 and unlike any 12-cylinder Ferrari (or the Dino V6 which sounds a lot like a 12). The exhaust tone is the epitome of the word guttural. It's not unpleasant but it's not a rich sound either – until you get up around 6500–7000 rpm. Then it takes on a melodious tone that is unmistakingly Ferrari".

*Some confusion persists when writers use this term. The 308 has two cams per bank (double overhead cam) but is more precisely called a "four-cam".

How to Shop for a Used Ferrari

The first consideration is whether you really want a used one or not. The reason is that, first of all, if you plan to keep the car for a long time, say 10 years, and have a habit of keeping your cars in pristine condition, it may recover its original cost after 10 years.

Secondly, due to a little known peculiarity of the U.S. emissions laws – where the emissions system must be operating for up to 50,000 miles, – many more things on the 328, bought new, are covered by the warranty if you can argue that they are "emissions-related." Thus, in effect, Ferrari has to give the U.S.-spec cars a 50,000 mile warranty, which isn't spelled out on paper, but is a beneficial side effect of the emission law. (Of course, if you remove your catalytic converters, you endanger any such coverage, plus are liable for $10,000 fine from the EPA!).

But, if a new one is simply not a viable path for you, then the next choice is a used one.

The Series I's

The earliest 308's are the GT4's, built by Bertone. These are among the best performers, in that many were built before catalytic converters were required and thus can run low-restriction exhausts legally. They also have a generous amount of room in the cabin – especially if only two people are in the car.

The disadvantages in the GT4's are that they lack any family resemblance to all the other 308's/328's, which are Pininfarina designs, and that many were stored outside during the winter of 1974 when there was a world oil shortage, so many had a good start on rust before they even arrived in America!

As far as performance, they can become 150 mph machines with only minor tuning done to the cams, carburetion and exhausts. In 1986, according to the *Ferrari Market Letter*, a low price for one was $15,900 and a high price $31,000.

The 308GTB & GTS

The first 308GTB's were fiberglass and these are collector's items now because they are about 200 lbs. lighter than steel coupé. But finding body spares might be difficult if you have an accident. But at least the body will never rust and some of these have the advantage of dry sump when the steel-bodied coupés imported to the U.S. were wet sump. The big advantage of dry sump comes in track work where the oil stays cooler longer – being located away from the engine, and there is less chance of some object piercing the oil sump because it is higher in the body than if it was under the engine as in a wet sump car.

The carburetored cars are simpler to service in terms of trouble-shooting as Weber carburetors have been basically the same for 40 years. But carburetors can also backfire if you run without the air cleaner, and cause a fire.

Still, if you work on the car yourself, the carburetored 2-valve 308 is the best to consider, because Weber carburetor technology is still relatively simple compared to fuel injection.

If you are considering a fuel-injected 308 of the first model year, try and find out if the engine is the original or a replacement. Ferrari of North America replaced over 100 engines when they had a porosity problem with the block casting but they may have missed a car. They might answer a telex confirming whether the car you are looking at has the original, or replacement engine.

The targas will *always* have more resale than the coupés, mostly because they are more attractive and because of publicity like worldwide exposure on the TV show *"Magnum P.I."* (and, because, if you are over six feet tall, like Tom Selleck, you need to take the roof off to have any headroom!).

So, given the choice between a very clean 308GTB and a somewhat neglected cosmetically 308GTS, I would take the "S" because it is a better investment.

As far as the QV's, not enough mileage has been accumulated yet for any flaws to show up, but ever since Ferrari has required to meet the 50,000-mile emissions test, their reliability has improved. The same general rule applies as to the open car vs, the closed one as far as resale. The open car wins.

What to Look For

Since many 308's were former rent-a-cars, and severely abused by their temporary owners during these periods of involuntary servitude, it is best to find a car still owned by the same private owner since new, and one who can document this fact.

Next, take the car to a garage and pay the mechanic to put it on a hoist. Check the main frame tubes to see that they both look alike and that there is no welding on one of them that indicates frame damage and a subsequent repair. Check to see if various brackets are missing bolts, nuts and screws underneath. If a car has been re-built hastily, sometimes a good bit of the hardware gets lost.

Do a compression check. It should be plus-or-minus 5 lbs. per cylinder. Check the oil. If it's low more than a quart, this car did not have a very attentive owner. Likewise if it is dirty.

Check the paint over for signs of overspray on the rubber. If a car is re-painted, there ***has*** to be a reason. The most common reason is an accident, though there were some 308's that were unsightly colors right from the factory and had to be re-painted in order to move them off the used car lots.

Check the tires (including the spare) for even wear. A tire really bald on one side with thick tread on the other half indicates a ***very*** severe problem, possibly a bent frame.

Subscribe to the ***Ferrari Market Letter*** and keep an eye on prices so you don't overbid. Offer to pay cash instead of a check (deliverable at a bank where he will hand over the keys and title in the lobby) for a discount.

Drive the car yourself. If there is something wrong with a car – like a slipping clutch – the owner can mask the flaw if he is driving. Drive it yourself so you can compare it with other cars you've driven.

When you take it to a mechanic, don't take it to the one the seller recommends, since he may have cued the mechanic to similarly mask the flaws. Pick out another one who is hopefully "neutral".

One special area of concern is the gray-market 308. In the late '70's, the gray market flourished and many were imported from Europe. Some of these are faster than the U.S. versions, but don't let that blind you to the "downside" of a gray market car, which is that there are some problems. To name a few:

- Some were never properly EPA-and-DOT tested, and converted. When you go to register it, the Department of Motor Vehicles may reject it – meaning you have to get it "converted" all over again unless you can provide the right EPA and DOT papers to convince them.

- Some European cars are rusty, since in Europe there is almost constant rain in winter.

- European cars have different bumpers, turn signals and even seat trim. If you damage the car, you may spend months trying to find matching replacement parts.

- Some European 308's were stolen and the numbers changed, whereupon they were imported to the U.S. With a U.S. car, Ferrari of North America can confirm its serial number. With a gray-market car, the history may not be documentable. The computers at the Department of Motor Vehicles in some states may "reject" your car's i.d. number as registratable.

Finally, it all comes down to condition. If you find for instance, a 308GT4, even if the 308GT4 doesn't have a "family resemblance," if you found one with less than 12,000 miles on it in clean dry storage, how could you resist? The point is that, where in real estate, the three most important factors are "location, location, location," in Ferrari 308's, the three most important things are "condition, condition, condition."

The clean, low-mileage one-owner car wins every time.

A Word about Depreciation

Much has been written about Ferraris being "good investments," and with the 12-cylinder models made in the 1950's and 1960's, this is certainly true. In fact, some models like the short-wheelbase 250GT's and 275GTB/4's were averaging 10 times their new car price at recent auctions and are expected to go still higher, far outdistancing most Wall street returns on blue chip stock investments.

But, according to the publisher of the bi-weekly Ferrari Market Letter (850, Maxey Hill Court, Stone Mountain, Ga.) one cannot expect the same of the Ferraris made after 1974. Even though the Ferrari factory, by 1987, could still only produce less than 4,000 cars a year, there are still too many Ferraris available for there to be any expected appreciation in the value of used 308's, Mondials and 328's.

The good news is that the depreciation will be very slow – maybe 10% a year if you buy a used 308 or 328. If you buy a 328 new, of course, just like a Detroit car, you lose about 1/4th of its value merely by driving it out of the showroom.

The Testarossa, though, went up in value so that Americans who bought it at its 1984 price of $85,000 were able to realize a profit a year later. So there is always the hope that, as Ferrari makes a wider variety of models, yet still stays under a total output of 4,000 cars per year, that there will be more demand-than-supply generated on *specific* models, causing used ones to keep their value or even appreciate as did the Testarossa.

We live in hope...

The 288GTO

Technically, the 288GTO deserves only a footnote in the 308/328 chronology because it is, after all, only a lookalike for the 308, not a derivation. The GTO was a specialized "racing" model made to be street-legal. It was announced in 1984 at a price under $100,000 but, as orders poured in, they were being bought and re-sold by entrepreneurs at twice that price.

The engine was a V8 but longitudinally-mounted instead of transversely, using a new 5-speed gearbox with a self-locking differential. The turbochargers are twin Japanese-made IHI units.

Originally, some magazine writers called it the "308GTO" but officially it was the 288 because its 90° V8 had a bore of 79.9 mm, a stroke of 71 mm and a total displacement of 2855 cc or 2.8 liters.

The engine was rated at 400 bhp at 7000 rpm, with 366 ft-lbs of torque at 3800 rpm.

The fuel injection was not by Bosch but by Weber-Marelli and microprocessor-controlled.

The body was pretty much derived of F1 car materials – overall it was fiberglass but the front and rear lids and roof were of Kevlar, a very light material.

The front and rear suspension were both different from the GTO. They both used parallel A-arms but Ferrari described them as "quadrilateral" A-arms since they were four-sided.

With a weight of only 2557 lbs. and all that power, the 288GTO's could go pretty close to 190 mph and had an odd whistle-like sound when both the turbos were wound up to speed.

When Ferrari first announced the 288GTO, it was thought that at least 20 would be built as all-out racing versions, but three years later, the racing version had yet to appear. And Ferrari showed great marketing skill in extracting maximum income from the 288GTO buyers by announcing that only 200 would be built. Each of the 72 buyers who bought cars after the 200th car probably thought he was getting the last one, as they could cut off production any minute!

The 288GTO was never street-legal in the U.S. but that didn't stop the ultimate Ferrari enthusiasts from trying – by hook or by crook – to Federalize one and one can see them on the road at various Ferrari events, wearing apparently legal license plates, emphasis on "apparently."

Problems

Road Test magazine was one of the first to report on it in print – the Ferrari clutch was a bit weak when used in the same brutal manner as, say, a Corvette clutch. One "burnout" or fast start off the line and *Road Test* had a burned-out clutch. How long *should* a clutch last in a 308? It all depends on the driving habits of the driver. The author, in 14,000 miles on a 308GTS, has a clutch that's not even showing signs of slipping yet. But there are reports of owners who can't go 4,000 miles without needing a clutch replacement, which in the U.S. can cost from $600 up.

One solution is to install a heavy-duty clutch from a Daytona. This lasts longer – especially if the car is to be used for racing but also adds tremendously to the pedal effort.

Some people want the opposite – a light clutch. Ferrari came out with a linkage kit in 1979 which could be installed to lessen the pedal effort. There is also a different pressure plate available that has support under the "fingers" which also lessens the effort.

Ferrari's philosophy of setting up the clutch changed in the middle of 1980. The older clutches had at least 5 mm of "free play" while the post-mid-'80 clutches have no free play.

An apparently insolvable problem with 308's is rapid tire wear. Michelins made their name in America as an after-market tire (not as original equipment on Detroit cars) when they created an image of being a 40,000-mile tire. On the 308's, that doesn't happen and most owners find the tread worn down in 6,000 to 10,000 miles. Since the 308 is independently suspended on all four wheels, it is important to have the rear wheels aligned when the car is new or uneven tire wear can be the result, so that you'll not even achieve the above-named mileage. One reason the wheel alignment is so often off is that it should be done with the car at "loaded height" – a full tank of gas and weight to simulate passengers. A car rides different when loaded than when empty.

Handling

Road Test magazine's testers, in their March, 1976 test, found that the GT4 understeered, but concluded this was forgiveable: "There are sound rationales", they wrote, "for an understeering car, chief among them that understeer is far less frightening to an inexperienced driver than the razor's edge control necessary in an oversteerer. In producing the Dino as an understeerer, Ferrari has clearly shown that it expects drivers of less than expert ability to own the car, and thus the handling characteristics are understandable, even laudable".

Paul Frère, described the handling at length of an early European model in their September 1974 issue. He found the handling: "typically Ferrari". He explained: "Even though their central engine cars use rack-and-pinion steering rather than the worm gear of the front-engine models, the people in Maranello have managed to retain that somewhat dead feel that has been a characteristic of Ferraris for more than two decades. You may like it or not, but the friction damping introduced certainly reduces kick-back more than is usual with a rack-and-pinion mechanism, and the control is very precise with good self-centering as soon as the car gathers speed. Though it's far from finger-light, the steering never becomes very heavy, but maneuvering is really hard work because of the appalling steering lock. I would also favor higher gearing because the 3.5 turns from lock-to-lock would correspond to 4.5 or more with a decent turning circle".

Paul Frère also felt that the handling at speed was exceptional: "When cornering, the typical Ferrari understeer is evident, but the faster you go the less it becomes and there is a reassuring feeling of stability and safety in fast corners taken near the limit. Lifting off makes the car take a slightly tighter line just as it should, and straight-line stability is nearly perfect, the car showing little sensitivity to side winds. Quick changes of direction are effected without fuss, as you would expect with a low polar moment of inertia, but some of the inherent agility is lost by the low-geared steering. The expert deplores it, but it may be just as well for the normal consumer".

John Dormer, a GT4 owner from San Diego,

Calif. reflects the customer viewpoint, saying: "The GT4 is a solid, predictably handling car. It goes where you point it with great stability and provides just the right amount of understeer to make a so-so driver look like a pro. If pushed very hard in a turn, the rear of the car moves out but the transition is smooth and controllable and it still responds promptly and smoothly to steering imputs. The intelligent use of the throttle at high 'slip' angles rewards the driver with truly fast and exciting cornering."

The Porsche 911 vs. Ferrari 308 comparison is something many auto magazine editors came naturally to when driving the GT4 including Britain's *Thoroughbred & Classic Car.* In their June 1982 issue, they compared a '77 911 with a '74 GT4 and found the Ferrari steering more of a workout: "In the Ferrari, fitted with less-embracing seats than the Porsche, you have to adopt an arms out knees-up driving position as in most Italian cars. Because the steering is surprisingly low-geared and the wheel not as upright as the Porsche's, drivers who normally sit well back have to lean forward and twirl vigorously to negotiate sharp corners. Parking and U-turns call for even more strenuous effort, exacerbated by a very poor lock."

But the magazine forgave the 308 everything for its performance out on the open road: "the Ferrari is pretty well everything you'd expect, at its magnificent best on fast sweeps; since an open roundabout constitutes a 'fast sweep' in a 308, it's evident that this is a car you simply aim through corners rather than steer round them, with nothing so rude as roll or tyre scrub, let alone instability to deter very spirited cornering."

Although the riding quality of the 308 GT4 is stiff, it was appropriate for the car's purposes, and many magazine road testers commented on it.

Paul Frère, commented in 1974: "the most outstanding feature of the Dino 308 is the excellent ride it provides. There is no low-speed harshness and at speed the road irregularities are beautifully smoothed out, damping being so good that oscillations are virtually non-existant, though passengers never become aware of the powerful dampers and praise

must go to Koni as well".

Road & Track's California-based editors, in their later 1975 3-car test done in the U.S. also praised the ride, which they found: "superb: firm and well controlled but wonderfully supple with rough road and dip taking ability belying its limited suspension travel. There's none of the front end bobbing over gentle undulations characteristic of mid-engine cars with the largest portion of their mass centered between the wheels".

Road & Track also commented: "the Dino sets new standards for comfort and outward vision in a mid-engine GT. Although the least stylish of the three (the comparison included the Urraco and Merak) its obvious that Bertone expended great effort to make the Dino interior a comfortable place to be. Only the Bora with its hydraulically adjustable pedals and multi-position steering wheel approaches the comfort available to a Dino driver. The seats have just the right amount of curvature and provide ample lateral support, the padded steering wheel and pedals are ideally positioned, instruments are large and readable and major controls such as lights, washer and wiper are on steering column stalks".

The rear seats, however, in all three of the mid-engine cars they tested were "ludicrous." *Road & Track,* went on:

"Those in the Dino are at least properly and reasonably comfortable for short distances if the front seaters co-operate by moving their seats forward, something we can't say about the severely upright rear seats in both the Merak and the Urraco".

But still, there remained lapses in the "creature comfort" area, some fairly embarrasing on a $25,000 car.

Paul Frère, in his 1974 road test was one of the first to pinpoint the inadequacies of the ventilation system: "Warm weather ventilation should be alright, but in cold or cool weather there is no alternative but to be cooked or frozen. I tried every combination for regulating the flow of water through the heater element and the flow of air without ever achieving the desired result". The heater operation never really improved in the GTB/GTS models from that in the GT4.

308 GT4/LM No. 8020

The first racing 308 was a GT4, built by the factory out of the first GT4 to be a Group 5 car for Le Mans in 1974. Just about everything on the car was changed, starting with the engine, which had Daytona pistons and rods installed, and the crankshaft and cylinders were machined so as to allow for slightly larger clearances. The heads were given a hot-rod style "port and polish". The exhaust valves were X-rayed to detect any hidden flaws.

Carburetion was still four two-throat Webers, but with 42mm venturis. With race cams and headers, the engine produced an estimated 300 bhp at 8200 rpm – not that big an increase, but the engine had to live at that rpm for 24 hours! The oil pressure bugaboo was handled with reworked oil pan baffling.

Because Le Mans requires good braking as well as acceleration, No. 8020, also had a brake change to Girling 4-pot calipers, DS11 competition pads and the master cylinders, linkage box and hoses from a racing 512. Brake cooling hoses were installed to feed cold air to the brakes, with scoops projecting out from the rear rocker panels to feed the rear brakes.

The suspension was beefed by replacing the rubber-based bushings with rigid ones, and installing larger diameter front and rear anti-roll bars. The tires, on modular wheels, were Goodyear 8" × 15" in front and 10.5" × 15" in the rear.

Copying the lightweight Daytonas, the doors were replaced with aluminum, as were the front and rear deck lids. All the glass except the windscreen was also replaced with light plastic, and the result was a car that, even with 40 gallons of fuel on board, weighed 2350 lbs compared to 2536 lbs. for the production European spec. 308 GT4.

The Group 5 rules then were fairly liberal regarding aerodynamic modifications, and among the mods performed on the car were an extended elevated Can-Am type adjustable wing, and rearward facing rear decklid scoops to feed cool air to the engine compartment (hot air ducted out through louvers).

The top speed of No. 8020 was 283–286 km/h, which translates to 176 mph.

In spite of that capability, the car didn't finish at Le Mans in 1974, its first year in competition, reportedly because of clutch problems. The car was taken back to Le Mans in 1975 by Luigi Chinetti's NART team from America but, after a dispute about whether it should be classed as a Group 5 GT car or a sports prototype, the car was withdrawn. The French were doubtless disturbed by the car's excellent practice times, which had put it in the front half of the starting grid.

The car was then taken back to California by owner Bill Schanbacher, where it has been campaigned extensively since in Ferrari Owner's Club events, from the annual Virginia City hillclimb to events at Laguna Seca and Riverside.

308 GT4/LM, the "LM" the designation given all Ferraris that race at Le Mans, demonstrated to Californians as early as 1974 that the 308 had great potential as a combination race/street car.

On the racing GT4, surprisingly little engine ventilation was needed—just four rows of louvers, and these two rearward-facing scoops.

The gas fill system employed on the GT4 was the modern "dry break" type—it doesn't need the cap removed to fill it. Note unusual push-button door lock!

The Rainbow Alternative . . .

Bertone didn't give up even when Ferrari announced the two-seater 308 design would go to their arch-rival Pininfarina. Indeed, they had their own two-seater spyder version waiting in the wings, built on chassis no. 12788 and code-named Rainbow.

The Rainbow, first shown in Turin in 1976, has to be one of the most wedge-shaped automobiles ever built, matched only by some of Giugiaro's show cars. The taillights were great flat planes of plastic, reminescent more of a Ford Thunderbird than any Ferrari past or present. The general shape was something like Bertone's wedge-shaped Fiat X1/9 design *writ large*, but it wouldn't have been good public relations to have a Ferrari looking like a Fiat.

About the only features worth thinking about on the Rainbow are the roomy no-nonsense interior and the unique way the metal targa top flipped down behind the two bucket seats, (though the top in the Pininfarina – designed 308 GTS isn't really *that* hard to demount, taking as little as 30 seconds).

Although Bertone designed it, the one-off body was crafted by Scaglietti of Modena (this before Scaglietti became Ferrari's in-house coachbuilder). The chassis was chopped 10 cm. in wheelbase and the Rainbow stands 16 cm. lower than the production GT4.

The slotted Speedline modular wheels were another abrupt departure from Ferrari tradition, and maybe something Ferrari – in their slow-moving way – will think about in the year 2000, but not at the present.

The Rainbow, unlike most other show cars, did not disappear after its three-year show career, but was actually put up for sale for a little over $100,000, which is less than half of what it costs to build a prototype in Italy these days. Whoever has it now has the distinction of owning a "one-off" Ferrari – a rarity indeed in this mass production world where the building of "one-offs" for private owners is a luxury even very small carrozzerias can no longer afford.

The interior of the Rainbow was a complete breakaway from Pininfarina's philosophy of stick-the-instruments-in-a-binnacle. The seats, with their under-the-knee bolsters, look more comfortable as well.

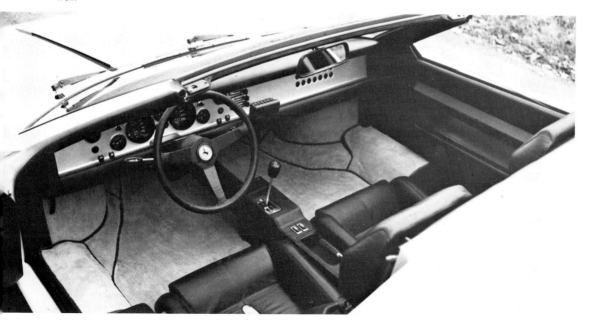

The Rainbow was more of a wedge shape than many of Guigiaro's designs yet Giugiaro "invented" the wedge. The squared-off front fender flares were also used on the production Lamborghini Silhouette, also done by Bertone.

From the back, the Rainbow did not look like any previous Ferrari, and the large taillamps looked like something you'd expect to see on a Ford!

From the direct front, the Rainbow at least looked Ferrari-ish but also a bit too much like a TVR or Lotus Esprit.

The High Cost of Keeping It Going

"It's not the buying of a Ferrari," some owners will say, "but the maintaining of it that *really* costs." This statement may not be applicable so much if one buys a brand new 308 and services it at the recommended intervals, but if one were to buy a used one – especially one with an uncertain past – the prices of service could be a shock.

In the U.S., a labor rate of $40/hr is charged by most independent foreign car repair shops, but "authorized" Ferrari dealers often charge $60 per hour for the same labor.

And, even though some "purists" might argue that the 308 "is not a real Ferrari," the prices for servicing it, and the parts, cost just as much as if it were a Daytona. In the U.S., the usual charge for tuning up a 308 at a "factory authorized" service facility is $1000. Even the parts used in a service call are extraordinarily expensive, such as the oil filter. Even though it is a Fram, made in America, the dealer charges from $22 to $40 for it. True, it is a special design with a "standpipe" in it to hold oil long after the engine has been shut off (so that when the engine is started cold, there is some oil at the top of the engine already). But it doesn't cost that much more to make than an ordinary $3 Fram filter. It's just that, once it goes through a Ferrari dealer's hands, it becomes a valuable commodity.

How often does a 308 need a tune-up? That depends on the individual owner's driving style and, whether, in the carburetored cars, he can keep his hands off the choke lever which would load up plugs. The author had only one tune-up in 14,000 miles on his 1979 308GTS and yet the car always started instantly and ran cleanly throughout the rev range. The fuel-injected ones need even less frequent tune-up so one could say that the old myth that Ferraris need constant tune-ups has been pretty well eliminated by the 308.

The Ferrari 308 engine, again, to counter the V12 elitists, is every bit as finely-made and fully machined as any of the previous Ferrari V12's (except, of course, for competition engines). It is, in short, a tool and diemaker's "dream engine," with every part balanced before assembly, and the tolerances adhered to in assembly are much closer than is acceptable in, say, Detroit.

But the 308 engine has proven to not be quite bulletproof – there are some things that prematurely wear out. Among them:

- *The Water Pump* – Whether it was the narrow drive belt that was too tight or a bearing that was too small, this pump gives out within 15,000 to 20,000 miles in '75–'79 308's. After that it was replaced with a new pump with a wider, taller, more heavy-duty bearing. This can be retrofitted to earlier 308's. Some private mechanics claim their reworked pumps are superior to the new factory design.
- *The Cam Belt's Idler Pulleys* – These rollers, which act as "chain tensioners" or, in this case, "belt tensioners", are unlubricated, and located outside the engine where they are exposed to sand and dirt. They rattle before they wear out however. In 1982 Ferrari came up with a sealed bearing roller that can be fitted to all 308s.

Lyle Tanner, of LTE Enterprises (20850 Leapwood, Carson, Ca 90746) an independent Ferrari parts source, cautions that the single most important part of the engine to look after is the rubber cam drive belts. "The factory says they can go for 18,000 miles but that's under ideal conditions. I would say replace them after 15,000 miles or as soon as the non-cog side looks worn. There's no clearance between the pistons and valves so you don't want this belt to start slipping. One slip and it's a valve job plus new pistons."

One of the most expensive service intervals in the 308's "life" is the one that occurs at the end of the first 15,000-miles. This is where the cam drive belts are changed, the head bolts torqued down good and tight, the carburetors taken off and boiled out, the gaskets and fuel filters changed, the valves adjusted and the spark plugs and points changed. Anyone who has skipped this key service process might be in trouble as soon as 20,000 miles. The price for this service can be as low as $650 at an independent shop to $1200 at an authorized dealer by 1982 U.S. prices.

Lance Nist, of Pantera Specialists, in Santa Ana, California, has worked on several 308's with water pump problems and believes that the main source of the problem is the tightness of the drive belt, which causes the pump to wear out prematurely. He replaces the thin belt with a much wider syncro cog belt on grooved rollers, which accomplishes the same thing but doesn't put so much pressure on the pump bearings.

Lance Nist believes that the chief inadequacy of the pre-injection 308's was the use of points. "Almost everyone else had gone to electronic ignitions," he points out. "The trouble with points is that Ferrari fires four cylinders off each distributor and, since the cam belts stretch minutely, your timing is always a little bit different with each engine revolution." Nist takes off one distributor, and replaces the other with an electronic unit developed for American V8's that is virtually bulletproof. "The engine revs up much cleaner and sharper with this fix," he says, pointing out that the conversion cost is approximately $500.

The authorized dealer frequently charges considerably more than a private service "on the outside" of the dealer network. One Southern California GTSi owner broke his windscreen and went to the authorized dealer for an estimate. The projected cost was $1,350 even though the part itself was listed as $420. The angry owner went to an ordinary auto glass store and got the same job done for $650 total, *including* the glass and labor.

Rust

One could call it "progressive de-materialization" but there's no disguising the fact that nature will have its way with steel and iron and somehow nature seems to wreak havoc on Italian cars with more of a vengeance than some cars from other countries.

In their 1982 look back at the GT4, *Thoroughbred & Classic Car*, in England, commented that: "Ferrari sheet metal rusts just like anyone else's – and the 308GT4 is nothing like so rot-proof as the Porsche, or for that matter its plastic-bodied 308GTB successor."

There are more rusty GT4's simply because they have been in production longer, and thus had more exposure. Although Ferrari wouldn't admit it, during the Energy Crisis of '74-'75, when sales were down, many GT4's sat outside in storage for months, which didn't help the rust situation.

The fiberglass body was a brilliant answer to the problem in the first GTB's but that turned out to be a short-lived solution. It wasn't until 1982 that Ferrari began to brag about their rust-control methods, and that was only in the 512BBi brochure, but one can assume that the 308's, Mondials and 400's all get the same treatment since they are built on the same assembly line. The treatment includes many coatings to prevent dissimilar metals (steel and aluminum, for example) from beginning a corrosive situation when joining each other, a common fault on Italian exotics for decades.

Perhaps the biggest help in eliminating causes of rust was the dropping of the practice of stuffing sponge rubber in nooks and crannies to prevent rattles. The sponges would soak up water and rot cars out from the inside. The GT4's had some sponge, but the GTB & GTS's have eliminated it.

Another myth attendant to exotics is their reputed excessive fuel consumption. Yet the 308 GT4 can earn 13 to 18 mpg even with occasional bursts of speed to 100 mph. *Motor* even reported earning 25 mpg in the GT4 by driving it "gently" but a Ferrari driven *that* gently seems to be a contradiction in terms. Suffice to say that fuel mileage in a 308 is roughly one-third better than that of a V12 Ferrari. While in America, where gas hovers around the $1.40/gal. mark at this writing, fuel mileage is still not as important as speed capability to a *Ferraristi*, in Europe petrol is closer to $5/gal., and *any* fuel saved is significant.

What the 308 GT4 did was introduce the world – particularly Americans – to a whole new class of Ferrari that dispelled a lot of old myths. For instance, to the uninitiated, Ferraris have the reputation of being temperamental cars, i.e. both hard to start and keep running. But if one follows the proper procedure – merely turning the key a half-turn first so the electric fuel pump can get some fuel to the carburetors – and holding it there for 5 to 15 seconds before turning it all the way, the car starts right up. (The fuel injected car is even quicker to start).

Foreign exotics – particularly Jaguars – always have a reputation for over-heating in traffic. With the twin electric thermo-statically-actuated cooling fans of the U.S. version of the 308 GTB/GTS, this doesn't happen. Even in rush-hour traffic with the air conditioning on, it would take at least 95°F ambient air temperature to push the coolant temperature into the danger zone. (A simple "save" in this circumstance would be to take the load off by shutting off the air conditioning).

The 308 GT4 had two, mid-engine rivals when it was first introduced – the Maserati Merak, powered by a quad-cam V6 – and the Lamborghini Urraco PlII, powered by a quad-cam V8. All were within $1000 of each other's price on the U.S. market and all could top 124 mph, though in *Road & Track's* test, the 308 GT4 was the fastest at 138 mph.

But Ferrari eventually "owned" the exotic mid-engined car market in the U.S. and the U.K. if only by default because the competition abdicated by promulgating uncertain production/distribution policies. Maserati went under once before DeTomaso took over the helm in 1975 and Lamborghini has sunk into a defunct status at least twice since then – each time to bounce back with new owners. It looked for a time that the Targa-topped Silhouette version of the Urraco might make for a good rival for the 308 GTS but that model has been phased out with the Lamborghini Countach taking up all their work force's time. At this writing, the Jalpa, an up-dated Silhouette, is being marketed as a revival of their V8-powered brother to the V12 Countach but in such limited quantities as to constitute no threat to the 308 GTS.

More's the pity, for the absence of any worthy rivals allowed Ferrari to sell the GT4 in essentially the same configuration for five years without any great updates or modifications such as might have been necessary had worthy competitors been threatening its market.

The Bertone era ended at Ferrari in 1980, when the last GT4 was built.* As Bertone is now more closely identified than ever with Ferrari's rival Lamborghini – it is unlikely that they will receive an opportunity to design a Ferrari again in the near future, making the GT4 stand out as that much more of an "odd duck" in the Ferrari family tree.

John Dormer, a 308 GT4 owner from San Diego, California, comments on the value in mid-1982. "The GT4 was initially a very difficult 'sell.' It suffered badly on the used car market for several years until the small number of really knowledgeable Ferrari driver/enthusiasts got the word out that the car was, in fact, a helluva fine car at a bargain price. Selling prices have since escalated rapidly and I predict the GT4 will become a very desirable machine with excellent resale value."

Any collector of virtually any finely-made object from Purdy shotguns to Leica cameras can tell you that it is the first and the last of a given series that appreciate faster than the ones in the middle and, since the GT4's are the *first* of the 308's, they should acquire intrinsic collector value eventually. Considering one can pick one up for 1/3rd the price of a Mondial 8, and yet have a faster car, they are definitely worth looking into. . . .

*Some were not sold until 1981, which leads to the confusion over model years.

TECHNICAL SPECIFICATION

GT4 U.S. version, [European version]

Engine
Type — 4-Stroke petrol water-cooled
Configuration — V8 cylinder inclined 90°
Bore — 81 mm — 3.19 cu.in (208:66.8 mm)
Stroke — 71 mm — 2.79 cu. in (208:71 mm)
Capacity — 2926.9 cu cm — 178 62 cu. in (208:1991 cu in.)
Compression ratio — 8:1:1* [8.8:1] — (208:9:1)
Horsepower — 205 at 6600 SAE Net [255* at 7700rpm]

Cylinder Block
Description — Silalumin casting with axis of cylinder bores inclined 46° from vertical when viewed from flywheel end.
Crankshaft — Steel forging with integral balance weights. Five main bearings.

Cylinder Head
Valves — Silalumin alloy, hemi-shaped combustion chambers Overhead with direct operation through inverted bucket type tappets
Camshaft — 4 overhead camshafts driven by cogged belt from crankshaft centerwheel

Lubrication
Type — Wet sump
Ignition
Distributor — Twin Marelli with contact breaker points [Single Marelli with contact breaker points]

Fuel System
Petrol tank capacity — 17.2 Imp. gal. 19.8 U.S. gal. 80 liters
Carburetors — Four Weber 40 DCNF
Choke — Manual
Air filter — Combined air cleaner and silencer with replaceable element.
Exhaust — Iron/aluminum four branch manifold
Fuel pump — Corona Electric
Electrical Equipment
Battery — Negative earth 12 volt
Capacity — 66 amps
Coding System — Pressurized "No Loss" cooling system comprising a sealed radiator mounted in front and a metal expansion tank in the rear.
Pump — Impeller pump
Fan — Two aluminum fans with viscous coupling. Electrically-driven. Thermostatically-controlled.

*Early U.S. version listed as 8.1:1 in brochures.
*Quoted as 240 bhp in early brochures.

Exhaust System   Twin mild steel down pipes from the manifold running into a transverse silencer with outlet into twin sets of tailpipes.

Transmission
Gearbox   Five speed all synchromesh with gate-type selector
Clutch   Diaphragm clutch with single dry plate hydraulically operated.

Ratios, gearbox

	1st	2nd	3rd	4th	Top	Reverse
	3.42	2.35	1.69	1.24	0.95	3.24
Overall	12.669	8.719	6.274	4.611	3.529	12.036

Rear axle   Independent rear suspension with constant velocity joints at transaxle coupling. Limited-slip differential.

Suspension
Front   Independent. Unequal-length A-arms. Telescopic shock absorbers and coil springs. Anti-roll bar.
Rear   Independent. Upper and lower unequal length A-arms. Coil springs. Telescopic hydraulic damper units. Anti-roll bar.

Wheels and Tyres
Wheels-type   Die-cast alloy wheels with flat rims. Five stud fixing.
Tyres-type   Tubeless radial ply
    Size   205/70VR14
    Pressures   30/34 (Michelin)
Brakes   Hydraulically-operated divided system by tandem master cylinders with front and rear discs. Mechanical hand-brake operating on rear brakes.

Front Discs Diameter   10.7"
Rear Discs Diameter   10.9"
Steering
Type   Rack and pinion
Wheel   Three-spoked dished steering wheel with padded rim.
Diameter   14"
Turns, lock-to-lock   3.3
Turning circle   39.3
Body   Two door four seater steel body of unitized construction built atop a tubular frame. Alloy front and rear deck lids. Safety bumpers front & rear.

Interior
Seating   Two individual reclining front seats with adjustable head restraints.
Upholstery   Leather. Moulded pile carpeting with driver's heel pad.
Seat belts   Inertia-reel harnesses used.
Interior equipment   Dipping rear view mirror. Passed sun visors. Cigar lighter. Clock. Interior light operated by door switches.

Electrical Equipment
Instruments and warning lights   Set into fascia panel in front of the driver. Speedometer calibrated to 180 mph* containing total mileage odometer. Tachometer 0–10,000 rpm, RED Line 7700 rpm.
Warning lights   Brake failure. Parking brake. Alternator. Low Fuel. Fan on. Rear window heater. Lights on. Hazard. High-beam. Directionals.

*Changed to 85 mph in U.S. models from 1979 on.

Controls and switches	Fascia-mounted heater and air conditioner controls. L.H. Drive stalk controls direction indicators. Fascia mounted toggles for fog lamps, warning flashers, defroster fan.
Horn	Twin Fiamm electrically actuated
Windscreen wipers	Twin electrically-operated self-parking rack driver windscreen wipers, black anti-glare finish. Electric pump-operated washer with plastic reservoir in engine compartment.

Lighting

Headlamps	Twin 5″ diameter retractable headlamps on each side, sealed-beam in U.S.
Wattage	[55]
Side lamps	Side lamps housed in front fenders
Rear lamps	Rear light cluster in rear valance panel with stop/tail lamps, reflectors, direction indicators and reversing lamps.

Heating and Ventilation

A heater/demister unit mounted in the dash panel incorporating a water-heated element delivers fresh air of required temperature to the interior and the windscreen. Variable direction outlets are located in the center of the fascia. Three-speed booster fan.

Acceleration through the gears	Secs
0–30 mph	2.6 [2.5]
0–40 mph	4.0 [3.6]
0–50 mph	5.7 [5.4]
0–60 mph	7.9 [6.9]
0–70 mph	9.3 [9.1]
0–80 mph	11.8 [11.4]
0–90 mph	17.8 [15.2]
0–100 mph	22.1 [18.0]
Standing ¼ mile	16.1 [14.9]

Maximum speed 138 mph (154 mph]
(Europen figures in brackets)

This constitutes a "mystery car." It says GTB/4 on the side—a designation the factory never used for the GTB. It has riveted-on fender flares all around, modular wheels, road lamps, twin gas fillers caps and racing harnesses for the single bucket seat. The pictures were taken in October 1977 by an American touring the factory. The factory denies all knowledge of this "works-built racer." (Hilary A. Raab Jnr.)

CHAPTER THREE

The 308 GTB/GTS

It had been rumored, of course, but there had always been rumors. "A short wheelbase coupe," they said. And, in the fuzzy spy pictures taken by cameramen hiding in trees, indeed it was.

But it wasn't like the GT4, that pig. No, it was low, and lean, like the Boxer, but somehow better. There was the scoop on the side, like the nostril of a snake, and the hint of a business-like spoiler below the nose, and a slight spoiler uptwist to the tail.

How big would the engine be? Three liters? Four liters? No one knew for sure, just as they couldn't say whether the body would be of steel, aluminum of fiberglass, or all three.

But it really didn't matter. The important thing was that the newest Ferrari was being designed back in the house of Pininfarina, and that it would be a pure 2-seater, a short-wheelbase berlinetta . . . almost like in the old days. . . .

The first 308 two-seater, the GTB, was welcomed eagerly by enthusiasts because the GT4, however many it may have sold, was not what one could call "an aesthetic success." As *Motor* magazine's Rex Greenslade commented: "The wedge-shaped GT4 lacked the sensual curves that one had come to expect of the normally Pininfarina-styled Ferraris, as well as the sharpness of handling that so seduced a 246 driver."

Perhaps the disappointment, too, stemmed from the fact that the 308 GT4 seemed an inappropriate follow-up to the Pininfarina-designed 246 Dino. According to Greenslade, though, "The GT4 was never meant to replace the 246 – the 308 GTB eventually did that." Yet Greenslade's hindsight fails to account for the fact that the 308 GT4 originally carried a "Dino" nameplate on the bonnet, and not a Ferrari one. Evidently, as far as Ferrari was concerned, it *was* a Dino.

The GT4 was phased out in 1980, even while the Pininfarina-designed 308 GTB was being produced. The fact that the GT4 was kept in production well after the two-seaters came into production in 1976 to fill the two-seater Ferrari "void" (the Boxer, although a two-seater, was in a higher performance category and higher price class), demonstrated that Ferrari felt that there was a need for a 2-plus-2. This need is inexplicable to American enthusiasts who, one feels, would rather have a "balls-out" performance machine (one thinks of the Daytona here) if it is going to wear the name "Ferrari".

The Styling

The styling of the new GTB was all "new," incorporating all the familiar Pininfarina cliches – the Boxer's dihedral line splitting the top and bottom; the 246 Dino's side air-scoops; the later Boxer's quad taillamps. It was, as GTB owner (and GM designer) Gerry Palmer says, "the more expected design." In short, a mini boxer, but perhaps a more modern interpretation; a Boxer with many of the shortcomings in packaging corrected, if you will (for instance, the addition of a trunk compartment where the Boxer had none other than the narrow space behind the two seats).

Michael Scarlett, *Autocar*'s Technical Editor, commented on the new body: "For what it is worth, I find it a far more pleasing-looking car than the Bertone 308. Pininfarina has returned here to some beautifully *right*-flowing curves, most refreshing after the somewhat anonymous flatter panels, more currently fashionable I daresay, of the Bertone 2 + 2. Admittedly, it is not easy to make such smooth curves in a 2 + 2. But whatever allowances one makes, the 308GTB looks like a Ferrari, every inch, and to me the 2 + 2 less so."

The mid-engine 'luxury GT' concept was experimented with well before the Boxer by Pininfarina, who built two "one-offs" ("two-offs"?) on 365P racing car chassis in 1966 and 1967. The really odd thing about these cars was the centrally-mounted steering wheel. The engine was a V12 mounted longitudinally.

The "dihedral" groove dividing the top half of the car from the bottom is seen in this view of the 365P. The car influenced both the 246 and the 308 series.

Here is the other 365P built in 1967, following the earlier version without the rear spoiler. Influences on GTB/GTS can be seen in rear fenders, air intake scoops, rear 3/4 windows, and fender air intakes.

The 308 GTB/GTS profile was also predicted back in 1967 in Pininfarina's one-off Dino berlinetta—actually one of their Fiat Dino roadsters with a top tacked on. If you imagine the rear 3/4 window about half its side, and a groove cut into the body at the "beltline," then you have the GTB/GTS. Pininfarina didn't get the contract for the coupe version, though—that went to their arch-rival, Bertone.

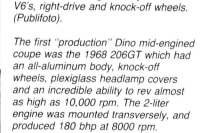

The Ferrari 206SP was the ancestor to the 206GT and 246GT production Dinos. It is remarkable how many of its styling features were picked up in the GTB/GTS; the rear fender air intake scoops and the shape of the fenders. The 206's had longitudinally-mounted V6's, right-drive and knock-off wheels. (Publifoto).

The first "production" Dino mid-engined coupe was the 1968 206GT which had an all-aluminum body, knock-off wheels, plexiglass headlamp covers and an incredible ability to rev almost as high as 10,000 rpm. The 2-liter engine was mounted transversely, and produced 180 bhp at 8000 rpm.

Much more of a production car was the 246GTS, the open-top version of the steel-bodied 246GT coupe. Its 2419 cc transverse V6 produced 195 bhp at 7500 rpm. It didn't rev as high as the 206GT but was a much more useable car in terms of daily use. Note change to 5-lug wheels, and uncovered headlamps (covered lamps are illegal in many countries, including the U.S.)

The vents over the headlamps is not something new at Pininfarina. In 1969, they used a smaller version of the GTB/GTS fender vents on their one-off "Berlinetta Speciale" 512/S show car, based on a Ferrari race car. Rear fender air intakes are huge.

Pininfarina realized the problem of daytime "flashing" (to signal when overtaking) without foglamps in the GTB/GTS. Their experimental GTB had large road lamps fitted into the grille cavity with a few vertical bars missing. The full-width bumper has been converted to two bumperettes similar to the '71 Panteras.

45

The 1969 Alfa 33-based Pininfarina show car also had previewed the GTB/GTS, particularly in the rear fender lines, the air scoops on the sides and the relationship of the front fenders/hoodline. Take out the T-roof bar and add "blind" sail panels and you would have a shape close to the GTS.

The experimental 308GTB was built in 1977 but already had the TRX wheels—with their outward-projecting center sections. The deep front spoiler was shown in aluminum, and both the front and rear fenders had flares added to accommodate wider wheels and tires. Barely noticeable is the front bonnet air grate, similar but not identical to that used five years later on the 208 Turbo.

This 1977 Pininfarina picture of the forthcoming 308GTS is significant for two reasons—it shows that they were considering having both the rear 3/4 window slats and front fender vents painted black. Private owners frequently do the same to their cars.

What happens to old prototypes? Well, in this picture taken in May '78 outside the factory we see the Pininfarina '77 show car parked between old tires and smashed cars. (Hilary A. Raab Jnr.)

Instruments

Pininfarina continued the practice of having one stalk doing everything – lifting the lamps into place and changing from low to high beam with a twisting maneuver of the stalk. But in the GTB, the lever doesn't work logically and it is all too easy to be plunged into darkness with a wrong turn of the lever. Fortunately, for overtaking flashing, a mere pulling back of the stalk with one finger (only if the lights are up) puts on the high beams.

The exterior was not only all new in the 308GTB but so was the interior. Once again, as in the 206/246 Dino, the instruments were squeezed into a narrow hooded nacelle. But, in this case, Pininfarina designers might have gone *too* far in creating a stylized look, for they found they had no room left for two dials – the oil temperature and the clock. These "left-over" gauges were then mounted to the left underside of the dashboard where it took a conscious effort of the driver to find them. Originally, the Veglia gauges all were inserted into a brushed aluminum surface, matching

the steering wheel spokes, but both were changed in 1980 to a black surface, perhaps because some felt the all black theme gave more of a "competition" look.

Among the areas where the GTB/GTS models are truly marginal is in the lighting of the instruments. Traditional white-on-black gauges may look great in the daytime, but at night it would be nice to have a little light thrown onto them. Ironically, the green light that lights up the central console is far too bright – so much so that this author on his own GTS habitually drives with his hat over that light. Volvo long ago pioneered the use of gauge needles being painted with reflective paint lit from above, and Toyota, on the 1982 Supra, have truly leapt into space-age instrumentation, but somehow Ferrari's GTB/GTS gauges are still back there in the days of light-a-match-to-read-them-Luigi. A particular annoyance on the American-spec 308's since 1979 was the 85-mph speedometer thought up by some dim-bulb at the DOT who thought it would prevent hot-rodders from driving beyond that speed. (The old one read to 180 mph.) All it means in a Ferrari is that, after you upshift from second at redline, the speedometer has ceased to be functional. Fortunately, pipelines exist in the U.S. to supply 180-mph speedometers that can be installed in minutes and give a driver something to shoot for. Fortunately, in mid-1982, the U.S DOT rescinded that requirement, so all that remained was for Ferrari to put the old speedos back into the pipeline.

The early ('77-'78-'79) GTB's and GTS's had the oil-temp gauge and clock to the driver's left where it was almost impossible to see at a glance.

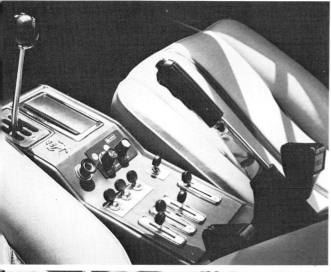

Pininfarina's approach to switchgear was to take it off the dashboard and put it on the console—which led to a somewhat "busy" look. This is a '78.

In 1980, the gauges formerly to the driver's left were moved into the center, in a mini-console ahead of the shift lever. The new seat pattern was supposed to prevent the seats from being so slippery.

Among the changes on the '81 were the re-location of the clock and oil temperature gauge horizontally. The carpeted lower door panelling was offered from 1980 onwards.

Ferrari of North America found a use for the space when the clock and oil pressure gauge were moved from the left of the steering wheel to the console—they stuffed a Clarion graphic equalizer into the hole, and mounted a Clarion programmable AM-FM stereo cassette radio in the radio cubbyhole. This is a mid '82 GTS with the 85-mph speedometer in place even though the requirement for it had been invalidated in mid-'82.

This drawing, from the Bertone files, reveals that before the car reached the "clay" stage, a "kick-up" over the front wheelwells and louver-like ventilation slats were considered—ironically Pininfarina later used that idea on the 308GTS. (Drawing courtesy Bertone Carrozzeria).

The "styling study" by Pininfarina had riveted-on fender flares, a hood vent, a rear deck spoiler and extra-deep front spoiler. All were eventually adopted except the fender flares.

One of the really laughable things about the U.S. version of the 308GTB and GTS is the warning lights which the U.S. government legislated onto the dashboard. One reads "slow down cyl 1–4" and the other reads "slow down cyl 5–8". *Road & Track* commented: "While we understand that their purpose is to inform the driver if the catalyst for either bank of cylinders is overheating, they certainly conjure up a funny image: Drive the hot half of the engine easy and keep pushing the cool half!" But the result of ignoring the lamp was anything but laughable – the U.S.-spec car was designed to cut off the four cylinders over-heating the convertor. You could limp home but if you continued to press on at full throttle, even more damage could result. Oh, by the way, when you first start the car and the convertor lamps both flash at once for a second, that's just a "check" to show they're working.

While the white-on-black Veglia-Borletti gauges in a Ferrari are appreciated because of their "traditional" look, they are sometimes annoying in their function. The gas gauge is the worst culprit: since the 308 has two "side-saddle" gas tanks, the remaining gas on an emptying tank sloshes from one side to the other, giving you readings anywhere from "¼ full" to "empty" depending on the angle of the car at any given moment

An enthusiast not familiar with the way things are done at Ferrari can be excused for wondering why all new Ferraris come with Michelin tires when there are others on the market which are 1) stickier, 2) less costly, or 3) both.

Ferrari got its racing tires from Michelin, at a time when the other big suppliers of racing tires decided to abandon the field. Accordingly, Ferrari has been more inclined to consider Michelin's wares as standard equipment on their production cars rather than those of other tire makers, regardless of how the enthusiasts may feel about their choice. In the past for instance, when Firestone supplied Ferrari's Grand Prix tires, Firestones went on the street cars; when Shell supported the Grand Prix team, the factory publicity photos seemed always to be taken in Shell gas stations.

The tires offered originally on the GTB were Michelin 205/70VR-14 steel-belted XWX's – the same size all the way around. The European models had a very narrow width (Ferrari calls it "reduced section") tire called a "high pressure" spare, mounted on a special 3" wide cast wheel. This allowed a few odd bits of soft luggage to be squeezed in the boot atop the spare tire (at the risk of denting the alloy lid if you inserted too bulky an object!). But the American DOT must have taken a dim view of high pressure spares, as the American 308GTB's still required a full-size spare tire mounted on a full-size wheel which squeezed horizontally into a fiberglass tray with barely a millimeter to spare (in fact, in the author's own 308GTS, a leather belt is carried and the

In Europe, the 308 is available with what is called a "high-pressure" spare. Although it is on a tire only 3" wide, since it is inflated at almost double the pressure of an ordinary tire, it allows the car to be driven at a normal rate of speed to the nearest tire store. Unfortunately the U.S. DOT does not approve of such a novel idea—so U.S. buyers cannot order this option, which, of course, makes possession of it a status symbol among 308 owners.

passenger's strength relied on to help "jerk" the spare tire wheel loose from its fiberglass cubby-hole).

Back in 1970, Ferrari made the mistake of not designing the 365 Boxer for the new generation of lower profile 50-series tires that they knew were coming from Pirelli. This was a serious error, as the Pirelli P7 emerged as *the* outstanding performance tire of the 70's, and even was designated as standard equipment on such cars as the Porsche 930 Turbo and the Lamborghini Countach S. Belatedly, some German Ferrari dealers like Wolfgang Koenig introduced 16" tall wheels and other bits designed to allow the Boxer to be fitted with P7's, but at least Ferrari wasn't to make that mistake over again with the 308GTB and GTS. Even though the "official" tire that came standard with the car was the Michelin XWX (and later the TRX), there was a 16" wheel and Pirelli P7 option quietly made available which required special spring rates and rear camber changes designed to work with the Pirellis. One danger with P7's is that they are lower profile than Michelins and bring the chassis a little lower to the ground, thereby increasing the danger of grounding the car should the springs be compressed too far. (The *real* danger of grounding, though, comes from the deep spoiler that is standard on 308's ordered with P7's from the factory.)

The TRX Era

Michelin developed a new-generation tire on the principle of evenly-distributed stress (*Tension Repartie-X*), which gave the tire its name. The TRX tread pattern is composed of rows of precisely-sculptured "V"-shaped-blocks that function as "escape channels" for water. It's important for a high-performance tire to be able to shed water at a rapid rate to maintain its grip, and Michelin asserts that the TRX has this quality as a priority feature.

The challenge with adapting the TRX design to the 308 was that it required a specially-sized wheel. Michelin had found that, in a conventional radial, most of the flexing of the sidewall occurred outside and above the wheel flange, which was not really ideal, since the tire was depending on the strength of its sidewalls to carry the weight. Their solution

was to design a wheel with a "shallow rim flange" (flatter when looked at in side profile). This way the "flexing point" is above the metal part of the wheel, not outside it, widening the flexing zone more than a conventional radial and improving the stability of the tire overall because the flexing occurs over a solid "foundation" below.

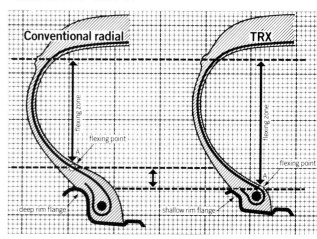

The TRX tire has its main flexing point over the wheels flange rather than almost outside the flange, resulting in a more consistently-feeling tire than the XWX. The TRX's even seem to make steering easier in the GTBi/GTSi series. (Drawing: Michelin)

Ferrari adopted a wheel with a lower, angled flange for all the 308's at the same time they went to fuel injection. But cars so equipped cannot be switched to other conventional radials should the owner decide to try something else. At this writing, only one other tire-maker makes a tire to fit a TRX wheel.

While TRX tires are offered on many other makes of cars, on the 308 Ferrari – a *very* firm-riding car to begin with – the effect of the TRX's can be felt immediately compared to a 308 fitted with conventional radial-ply tires. The feelings of being in control and stability are increased. The tires seem to track straighter as well, and one only pities the owners of more softly sprung cars who can't feel the improvements as directly as the Ferrari owner.

In their comparison between the 308, on Michelin TRX's, and the Lotus Esprit Turbo, on Goodyear NCT's, *Car* magazine felt that

52

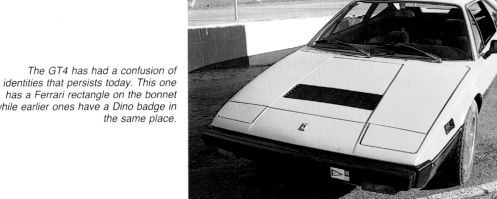

The GT4 has had a confusion of identities that persists today. This one has a Ferrari rectangle on the bonnet while earlier ones have a Dino badge in the same place.

The '78 and '79 308 GTS models were virtually identical, but the '80's marked the switch to TRX tires, and differently shaped wheels. This picture was shot at Riverside, California during a Ferrari Owners' Club event. Note racing GT4 and BB512LM in background—typical "hot" club racers.

It is often thought all European 308's came with the deep spoiler seen on this English model displayed at the annual FOC Concours. But, in fact, some European short–wheelbase cars have the short spoiler, which is less prone to damage on steep driveways.

The two-tone "Boxer"–paint scheme was first thought up by dealers who were having trouble selling GT4's. By 1981, it became a factory option. (K. Oblinger)

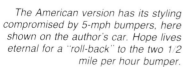

The American version has its styling compromised by 5-mph bumpers, here shown on the author's car. Hope lives eternal for a "roll-back" to the two 1/2 mile per hour bumper.

the Michelins weren't as grippy as the Good-years. "Despite the fine job that Michelin XWX tires have done on Ferraris for many years, these new TRXs take its chassis capability a biggish step further. True, it doesn't have as much outright grip as the Lotus, but it couldn't be more than a percentage point or two behind. What the Michelins seem to do for the Ferrari is to dramatically cut the old car's low speed tire noise and to further 'tune' the chassis breakaway characteristics so that they are utterly predictable and quite graceful. In the Lotus you feel that provoking any kind of breakaway goes against the inclination of the designers and the car itself, but in the Ferrari there is a kind of semi-slide, drifting condition which is beautiful, fast and down-right inspiring."

Driving the GTB & GTS

As in the GT4, the performance capability reported for the 308 GTB/GTS depended on the specifications for the country involved, and the redline observed by each magazine's test driver. In one of the earliest *Road & Track* reports (March, 1976), by Paul Frère of a European-spec fiberglass GTB, he reported a 0–60 mph time of 6.4 seconds and a top speed of 154 mph, turning 6900 rpm at that speed. Ferrari claimed a 147 mph top speed but some test drivers told *Autoweek* in 1977 that it would do 155 mph at 7700 rpm. None of the non-race driver road testers from other magazines ever got close to these figures, a fact which can be attributed to heavier cars, lower compressions, lower octane fuels and – let's face it – poorer driving abilities. (Frère was a veteran Le Mans competitor.) Yet another factor that's always present is the length of the test track (which may, in fact, be a length of public road.) Frère might have worked the GTB to 7700 rpm in fifth but the length of road needed might not be found outside of Bonneville, Utah.

When *Road & Track's* U.S. editors had an opportunity to test a U.S.-specification 308 GTB, the figures were less impressive – a 0-to-60 mph time of 9.4 seconds and a top speed of "only" 132 mph at 6350 rpm. Although these figures are for a GTB, *Road & Track* claim that the GTS weighs only 50 lb.

more than the coupe. They must have been talking about the steel coupe, for Frère, in his original test, quoted an unbelievably light curb weight of 2650 lb. for the European-spec fiberglass coupe in 1976 while *Road & Track* claimed 3300 lbs. for the steel-bodied U.S. version of the GTB/GTS in 1978.

The irony of the 308 in its American version was that, in going from the carburetor version to the injected version, it lost approximately 14 bhp but never lost any weight. So the car became slower and slower. The turbocharger developed for the 208 in Europe and the 4-valve head first tried on the European Mondial 8 in 1982 will doubtless be good cures for this "creeping senility" but, meanwhile, the 308 in America was getting the unfortunate reputation of not being a very quick car.

A word about the "S" in GTS . . .

Ferrari called the 308 Targa, introduced at the Frankfurt Show in 1977, the "GTS" like their earlier 246 GTS. "Targa" is a model name formally registered by Porsche (emanating from their participation in the famed Targa Florio race in Italy). The "S" designation means "spyder" or "open car" in the original Porsche sense when, back in the '50's, they produced several mid-engine open racers called "spyders." But the origin of the word "spyder" in relation to cars gets a little obscure from there on, possibly originating from the days of carriages, when a very light in-town carriage with elegant thin wheels was known as a "spyder." Perhaps the first open sports cars were also light and elegant, giving rise to the name.

But the use of the "S" to designate an open car is not universal in Europe, where the Pantera GTS and Porsche 928S are both closed coupes, the "S" designation here presumably meaning "Super" since both cars have strengthened engines and chassis compared to the "normal" models.

Interestingly, when a German Ferrari dealer began offering 308's cut down into *full* spyders, with folding soft tops in 1981, he called it the 308 *Convertible*, that word evidently applying universally to cars with folding soft tops.

Inspiration, Circa 1972 . . .

The beautiful design of the 308GTS may be one of Pininfarina's best but perhaps not one of their most *original* creations.

For one only has to dig through the archives of the Torino Auto Salon to find that, in 1972, one Francis Lombardi displayed a car called the FL1 which, proportionately, strongly suggests the 308GTS.

Even the physical dimensions are surprisingly alike:

	308GTS	FL1
Wheelbase	2340 mm	2420 mm
Overall length	4230 mm	4214 mm
Overall width	1720 mm	1700 mm
Overall height	1120 mm	1135 mm
Track, front	1460 mm	1400 mm
Track, rear	1460 mm	1440 mm

Of course, the FL1 had only a 2-liter four-cylinder 125–6 bhp engine, while the 308GTS has, of course, a 3-liter V8. But both had near the same weight distribution – 44% front /56% rear for the FL1 42% front/ 58% rear for the 308GTS.

Did Pininfarina's stylists knowingly copy the FL1? Let us say "Great minds run in the same channels." Or "Imitation is the sincerest form of flattery" or . . .

The FL1 had the same downward-slant profile as the later GTB/GTS designs by Pininfarina. According to the drawings, the roof was not removable, but probably could have been designed to be so. The biggest difference between it and the Pininfarina design was the lack of tapered-back sail panels and the wrap-around horizontal taillamps rather than the circular ones favored by Pininfarina designers.

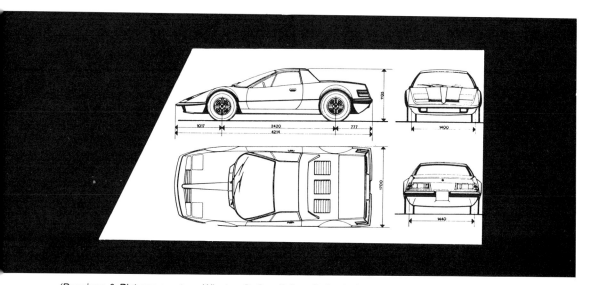

(Drawings & Pictures courtesy Winston S. Goodfellow Collection).

The old legend about Ferrari cranks being carved out of a solid billet is now an old legend as far as 308 cranks are concerned. Here's one day's supply at Maranello. (Motor)

The crank rides in five main bearings. Surprisingly, the hold-downs are two-bolt not four. (Motor)

The blocks are forged by Ferrari right at Maranello and receive a lot of machining to be approved for installation. (Motor)

Each engine is assembled by one mechanic on an engine stand and later tested. Ferrari doesn't go for the mechanic signing his name like Aston Martin. (Motor)

The view of hundreds of 308 engines makes them seem rather common, a "dime a dozen", when in fact they are worth more than $10,000 apiece. (Motor)

The Ferrari assembly line moves at about 1/10th the speed of a Porsche assembly line but virtually everything is installed by hand. (Motor)

Handling

Motor's August, 1978 comparison of the 308 GTS to the 911SC Targa (appropriately titled: "A Tale of Two Targas" . . .) was one of the most revealing comparisons ever made of the handling of two legends. Their collective opinion was that, 99% of the time, the Porsche can be pushed to the limit safely, but that when pushed too far too much of the time, the driver will find it has what *Motor* calls a "fundamentally unsound layout." *Motor* editors were careful to qualify that the point at which one loses adhesion in both cars is far beyond ordinary driving "simply because the limits are so very high, beyond the point at which most drivers' nerve runs out." Their opinion seemed to be that the Ferrari was more confidence-inspiring than the Porsche above 100 mph or nearer the limit of adhesion, though at normal speeds, the Porsche was "more rewarding to drive." This is an opinion the author would have to agree with, having driven both.

Motor's testers also drove the Porsche 911SC in the rain where they found "it demands more than respect, for the tail will all too easily step out of line, even under gentle acceleration." They did not drive the Ferrari in the rain but expected it to be better. This writer *has* experienced aquaplaning of the XWX's even when hitting shallow puddles in the rain at cruising speeds, but at least hasn't suffered a loss of traction while accelerating in the rain.

The 308 is a safe-handling car, even when one is so imprudent as to lift off in a corner. Peter Robinson, of Australia's *Sports Car World*, reporting on the testing of a 308GTS reported: "We tried provoking it by accelerating hard through a tightish corner in third gear and backing right off in the apex but this did no more than tighten up the line by tucking the nose in. Booting the accelerator hard in second gear in the same position in a corner can produce a touch of oversteer on dry roads but the opposite lock required to counter it is no more than a flick of the wrists."

Robinson also tried the car in the wet, and found it still controllable: "In the wet such brutal applications of power can produce larger oversteering slides but they are equally as easily controlled simply by backing off the accelerator. Once the driver understands the grip the Ferrari has, he will soon learn to steer it on the throttle almost as often as by the steering wheel, such is the rhythm it achieves through a series of sweeping bends."

The Porsche 911/Ferrari 308 comparison came up again in one of first 308GTB driving impressions published in the U.S., in the Dec. '76 *Road & Track* where they quoted Bob Bondurant, the ex-Cobra driver who campaigned for Shelby in Europe in 1964, and is one of the most well-respected race driving instructors in the U.S. The magazine arranged for him to drive one of the first fiberglass 308GTB's in the U.S. in 1976 (though the car was fitted with non-standard Pirelli P7's, sized 225/60VR15 on 15" × 8.5" BBS modular wheels which may have added immeasurably to his good impression of the car's handling.) Bondurant liked the car, making comments like: "With the 308, you can just drive and not worry about the car doing something unpredictable in the middle of a turn. I would say this would be a much safer car for the average guy to drive. It has very smooth weight transfer and transition in cornering . . . You get into a Porsche and they work fine up to a certain point and then they can go into an understeer or an oversteer; kind of snap oversteer. With the 308, even the guy who isn't quite as adept could take it that much closer to the limit."

Motor's staffers also noticed a drawback to the gearchange-clutch combination "(there was) a disconcerting tendency to (stick) on the floor on really fast changes: this may well have cost a couple of tenths of a second on acceleration times at the test track." Further, *Motor's* testers didn't like the action of the clutch. "In its action, the clutch is heavy, and its engagement somewhat abrupt – a characteristic that is shared by the 911 but aggravated by the awkward operating angle of the latter's pedal."

Even the layout of the Ferrari gearbox's five speeds is subject to criticism, depending upon an individual's preference as to which gear should be placed "outside" the normal "H" pattern. Ferrari believes it is first gear which belongs outside the "H" since first should only be used to start out. Once you're under way, you row around between second and fifth. Porsche, on the other hand, believes that the "H" should include first through fourth with fifth gear being relegated to the "outside" position because you only engage fifth out on the open road as a cruising or overdrive gear. As it turns out, if you live in a town with a lot of stop-and-go traffic, you will be using first gear quite often, at which time the "dogleg first" position favored by Ferrari "gets old in a hurry."

The externally-visible shift gate is as prominent in the 308 GTB as it was in the GT4 (indeed, a Ferrari's exposed shift gate is one of the few constants in the Ferrari berlinettas-and spyders of the last 25 years). But the shift linkage did not win universal praise. When Denis Jenkinson, the sage of *Motor Sport*, tested the 308 GTB in 1976, he wrote: "When I heard that the Ferrari 400GT was going to have automatic transmission I began to wonder if it would not be a bad idea for the mid-engined 308 GTB, for the gearchange on the five-speed box leaves a lot to be desired. The ratios are marvellous, and the clear and open gate are fine, but the movement is heavy and sticky, especially at low revs. When you have got it all wound on in third gear, the lever 'wangs' across into fourth all right, and 7,500 in fourth and a haul back into fifth is fine. But unless you are doing that, gear-changing is hard work and there is no encouragement to 'play tunes' on the lever."

Jenkinson hit upon something that few other writers have commented on – the controls seem bulky and uncooperative until it is driven at speed. *Then*, and only then, does it become a pure joy to drive. Unfortunately, in the U.S., with its 55-mph speed limit, the fact that the 308 does not "come alive" until you are doing at least 70 mph means that one has to break the law in order to enjoy it . This Jekyll-Hyde schizophrenia is maddening when one considers that there are other cars on the market – like the 500SL or Porsche 928S – that can be driven quite comfortably at low speeds, yet still allow one to enjoy the prospect of enormous performance capabilities at "top-the-ton" speeds.

The 308 GTB was only in production two years (if you count the European models as 1976 versions) before the Targa variant was introduced. Just as in the 246 precedent, it was named the GTS, and had a similar method of latching and lid stowage. Unlike the 246 GTS, though, the roof panel came in black imitation "leather-grain" finish where some 246 GTS models this author has seen have had roofs painted the same color as the body. (This can also be done to the 308 GTS by the private owner, but it requires considerable preparation to smooth out the top prior to painting).

With the introduction of the Spyder, Ferrari retrogressed to the wet-sump engine, even though most of the fiberglass European-model GTB coupes originally had boasted dry-sump lubrication. Presumably, this switch to a wet-sump was necessitated because of a lack of room for the dry-sump oil storage reservoir. Whatever the reason, it was enough to make some "purists" feel that the GTS was intended by the factory to be less of a performance car than the GTB, an impression reinforced when one drives the GTS down a bumpy road with the top in place and hears a steady squeaking caused by the flexing of the body in relation to this removable lid.

The two-tone "Boxer" paint theme became available officially in 1980, though some dealers applied it before that at the customer's request. This is a 1982 U.S.-spec. version

The wiring in a 308 looks complicated, but rest assured it's only half as complicated as that in a Porsche 928! (Motor)

Since Ferraris are assembled when already painted, great pains are taken to protect the finish, such as the covers shown here. (Motor)

The finished Ferraris are parked
outside if finished, but inside if they are
missing a few parts that didn't come
along at the right time during their trip
down the assembly line. (Motor)

The "i" means "injection" which is the
end of the Weber carburetor on
Ferraris—terminating a tradition since
the late 1940's

62

"European-Spec. – What is it?"	
U.S.-specification	European-market specification
—Front turn signal lenses in orange only	—Front turn signal lenses in orange & white or all white
—Back-up lamps in turn signal lens	—Back-up lamps in bumper
—Bumpers project out about 4"	—Bumpers project out about 2"
—Rectangular reflectors, front & rear fenders	—Circular turn signal repeater, front fender only, non-reflective
—Side door guard beams	—None
—Two belt-driven air pumps	—None
—Thermal reactor ('76)	—None
—2 3-way catalytic converters (after '77)	—None
—Full-size spare wheel & tire	—Narrow-rim high pressure spare with narrow tire or full-size spare
—180 mph speedometer ('76–'78) 85 mph speedometer('79–'82)	—280 km/h speedometer
—2 distributors (up to '80)	—1 distributor in carburetored car 2 distributors in "i" models
—None	—Alloy splash shield for distributor
—Short front spoiler	—Deep front spoiler
—Air conditioning std.	—Air conditioning optional
—Power windows std	—Power windows optional
—Leather standard	—Leather optional, cloth standard
—Automatic shut-off of ignition if car left idling for more than 30 seconds with no one aboard '79 only	—None
—English lettering on gauges	—Metric labels
—Wet sump on all cars	—Dry sump (on some '76, '77, '78 GTBs)

If the car you are looking at is *in* the U.S., and has more than three or four of the items in the right-hand column fitted, then it is best to ask for documentation proving it has already been certified by the DOT and EPA and is registerable in the U.S. before purchasing it.

The European GTB/GTS models have shorter bumpers front and rear than the 5-mph bumpered American-specification version (background).

One strange malady this writer found with his own 308GTS – and doubtless experienced by other owners – was its tendency to shut itself off if left idling for more than 30 seconds, or if too light a driver was aboard. It turns out that this was intentionally designed into the car as a safety feature, Ferrari figuring that if the car was to flip upside down and the engine was still running, the electric fuel pump would still be pumping fuel – probably all over the driver. The shutting off while idling while unmanned is only a minor inconvenience but the shutting off because the car judges that the driver does not weigh enough to be a driver is off-putting indeed. In fact, the only way my 80-lb. spouse could drive the car was to disconnect this device entirely (handy quick-disconnect plugs exist for this purpose under the driver's seat). Alas, this is another one of those "safety features" that looked good on paper but turns out to have been a major source of irritation to the driver in real life. This was discontinued in 1980.

The bucket seat used on the GTB/GTS is a primitive type – true, it has a recliner, but when you see inflatable lumbar supports on the Toyota Supra, it is obvious Ferrari is a little behind in seat technology. One particular problem with the seat is adaptability to beyond-normal size passengers. One 6' 4" driver had to remove the seat rails to sit in the car with the GTS top in place. One 4' 10" woman had to have special built-up pedals made to be able to operate her GTS. Ferrari makes less effort to make the car accommodating to different-sized drivers than do Mercedes, BMW and Porsche but then it's not because Ferrari thinks cars have to be uncomfortable to be true driving machines but because all those other cars are considerably taller. If the GTB/GTS were added to in height, it would certainly be more comfortable – but then it would lose much of its appeal.

Cool-weather driving

Ironically, what is good for a race car, or even for a very high-performance car, is not good for a street car. The Ferrari's cooling system is a typical example. With its large radiator, plus overflow catch tank, plus oil cooler, the Ferrari 308 runs too cool in a cold-weather climate. Capt. Terry Phillips, a weapon systems officer stationed in England, says of his 1979 European-specs. 308GTS: "I drive the first 11 mile of a 21 mile trip to the base on a 4-lane road, and although the water temperature comes up within 3–4 miles, the oil temperature takes 8 to 12 miles to come up to 60° Centigrade. Since I don't go over 3000 rpm until 60° C is reached or over 3500 rpm until 75°C is reached, the 11 miles of freeway is wasted on the way to work. On the way home, however, the car is fully warmed up and normal cruise speed is 4000 to 4500 rpm, which works out to 80 to 90 mph."

Capt. Phillips is even more bothered by the cold-blooded transaxle: "Before it is warmed up, the transmission will shift smoothly only if the clutch is absolutely fully depressed and slow deliberate movements are used. Shifting into 4th or 5th is particularly nasty with the transmission cold, and any shifting has to be done very deliberately. Once good and hot, however, shifts can be made very quickly providing one remembers to depress the clutch before starting to move the lever out of one gear detent before selecting another. A drag racing transmission it isn't, and it seems much more obstructive than either the Dino or Daytona I previously owned."

Ferrari could probably eliminate the oil cooler on all 308's going to cold climates, but a better idea would be to provide an adjustable cover for it, not unlike those used on diesel truck radiators when running in cold climates.

Fuel Injection

Starting with the 1980 models, all 308 models got an "i" affixed after the number "308," signifying "injection."

Whether the fuel injection was an improvement or not is immaterial – it was a necessity to meet worldwide emission standards (all that raw gas sitting around the float bowls of four dual-throat Webers just caused too many unburnt hydrocarbons to waft into the atmosphere!). According to those who have driven the car, the "i" versions run smoother. They have less "starting hiccups" and run without "coughing" if they are floored too early after starting out. One penalty of fuel injection was the loss of 14 bhp in the U.S. model.

Driving his Ferrari with great restraint, Andruet earned a well-judged victory on the 1981 Ypres 24 Hours. (LAT Photographic)

Prepared by Michelot and his Ferrari using Michelin tires and Total oils Andruet was expected to excel in the 1982 Monte Carlo Rally with the dry conditions prevailing. However the car immediately gave problems with a coil lead breaking then the brake pads not properly bedding in. (LAT Photographic)

The 1982 Tour de Corse car. (L'Auto)

While the factory never fielded its own racing 308GTB, it did apply for homologation, but only in its fiberglass form as a Group 4 car. The homologation papers included a roll bar structure, larger rear brake calipers, special exterior clamps to secure the rear roof lid, a special aluminum gas tank and various other parts, all of which had factory part numbers. However Group 4 was too tame a class for Facetti and Finotto of Italy, so they raced one in Group 5, where major body modifications were allowed. After a pole position of 121 mph at Monza, much was expected at the 129 mph Silverstone circuit in 1981. During the race it misfired with damp electrics and finally retired at half distance suffering a variety of electrical and transmission maladies. (LAT Photographic)

Where the European-market *carburetored* GTB/GTS models were definitely faster than the U.S.-specification models, the European-spec. fuel-injected models suffered a drop in horsepower when Ferrari went to fuel injection on the European 308's. *Auto Motor und Sport*, the highly-respected German automotive biweekly, was the only magazine worldwide that tested an "i" version that bothered to call attention to the relative slowness of the "i" model, when they ran a comparison of side-by-side test results in their No. 9 1982 issue.

	308GTS	308GTSi
0–100 Km/h	4.5 sec.	8.0 sec.
0–160 Km/h	14.2 sec.	14.9 sec.
0–200 Km/h	24.3 sec.	37.1 sec.
Top Speed	253. Km/h	226.4 Km/h

"The old power is gone without question and it seems that the factory-claimed 209 bhp (DIN) is very optimistic," commented *Auto Motor und Sport* "Even though the 308GTSi is still potent and full of temperament, it has lost its dominating role in the 3-liter class. A 911SC rated at 204 bhp (DIN) takes only 5.9 secs to go from 0–100 Km/h and has a top speed of 240 Km/h." Of course, while *Auto Motor und Sport* had a valid point regarding Porsches being faster than "i" 308's in Europe, U.S.-specification 911 Porsches are also much slower than in Europe, so U.S. Porsche owners don't enjoy the same clear-cut speed advantage.

Unfortunately, to meet the American regulations – which required the catalytic converter to be brought up to temperature quickly – Ferrari set up the American "i" cars so they idled at 2500 to 3000 rmp. This made those who knew about the amount of damage that could be done to a cold engine at high revs a bit tense, but the EPA dictates all in America.

There was also a rumor in America of a problem inherent in the first fuel-injected cars – something about the piston rings not being right for the high idle rate when the engine was cold. The result was premature scoring of the cylinder walls in many cars and Ferrari North America reportedly replaced a number of engines on warranty when the owners found themselves using up to four quarts of oil per every 1000 miles (normal rate is one quart per thousand miles). This problem may have since been solved but Ferrari declined to reveal to the author from what serial number the correction has been effected. Suffice it to say, by 1982 the complaints had lessened.

The performance of the fuel-injected cars also suffered somewhat due to the loss of at least 15 horsepower. *Motor Trend* tested a 308 GTSi in 1981, and reported a 0-60 mph time for 7.4 seconds and no top speed. Why no top speed? Simply because straightaways allowing 140-mph top speeds are not easy to find in California. They *did* report a standing quarter-mile time of 15.8 seconds at 87.7 mph which was the same elapsed time that *Road & Track* earned with a carburetored GTS the year before, though back then they reached 90 mph in the quarter.

The main reason for the switch to fuel injection was better emissions, because, in a fuel-injected car, fuel flow automatically shuts off during deceleration where in a carburetored car, unused fuel gathers in the float bowls of the carburetor(s), where some of it then evaporates into the atmosphere, adding to smog. But there are also mileage benefits from injection, and the injected 308's can return mileage as high as 20 mpg on an open road in fifth gear at the speed limit. While this is a big improvement over the V12's 9-to-12 mpg (for the six-carburetor Daytona), it is still not at all competitive in terms of what some cars like the Lotus Turbo Esprit or Porsche 944 can do. Both those four-cylinder cars can attain 140 mph like the 308, but both have the ability to earn well over 25 mpg when moderately driven, which the 308 can't. I suppose one could argue that, were Ferrari to build the 308 as delicate as Chapman builds the Lotus, they, too, would get good mileage, but such a change of philosophy isn't to be expected soon from Maranello, where robustness is recognized as a virtue.

If only the American-specification 308's were fitted with fuel injection, American enthusiasts would have good cause to feel further denigrated compared to most of the world's Ferrari enthusiasts who presently es-

The fuel injected engine has an even more complicated look than the carburetored engine. The tank on the left is for coolant, the black box on the right an air box for the oil cooler.

cape catalytic converters and other evils, but not only did Ferrari switch *all* 308's to fuel injection simultaneously, they also switched the 512 Boxer to fuel injection in September, 1981. If one first accepts the 512 Boxer as Ferrari's current ultimate supercar, then for the 308 to emulate the Boxer *must* be the correct way to go, n'est-ce pas?

The fuel injected 308's require more specialized equipment than carburetored engines in order to service fuel injection-based problems. Not all independent mechanics have up-dated their own stock of equipment to be able to handle diagnosing the K-Jetronic system. What this means to the used car buyer is that he may not be able to take it back to the same mechanic that serviced his carburetored Ferrari. Even if the mechanic buys a kit to check Bosch injection, a machine called a Gaftron ignition analyzer is needed to check out the Marelli Digiplex ignition.

How the Fuel Injection Works

Although the names suggests it uses a computer, the Bosch K-Jetronic system is mechanical and uses electronics only to operate the enrichment valve – to enrich the mixture for cold starting. Conversely, a bi-metalic strip, when heated up, leans down the mixture when the car has been running awhile.

Basically, the system is a continuous-injection system rather than a pulsing type. The spray feeds into the inlet tract leading to the intake valves. The fuel passes through a fuel accumulator first, then a filter, then to a mixture control unit that forms the core of the system. From there the fuel flows to the in-jector nozzles, one poised above each intake valve.

A key part of the system is an air flow sensor attached to a balanced and pivoting arm. The freedom of movement of the air flow sensor is also governed by the fuel pressure, activating a control plunger.

Every time the driver varies his pressure on the throttle, the sensor moves to change the air flow rate, and also the amount of fuel flow.

The importance of the fuel accumulator comes when cold-starting the car. The accumulator will delay the build-up of full pressure to temporarily reduce the pressure on the control plunger in the mixture control unit. When the driver shuts off the engine, the accumulator maintains the working pressure for a time to aid in hot starting (a problem with some carburetor cars, where vapor lock can occur).

The Marelli Digiplex electronic ignition uses a coil, a distributor head and an electronic module at the end of each bank of cylinders. The last-named device determines the correct amount of ignition advance to apply to meet variations in engine load and speed.

The engine load is determined from the vacuum in the intake manifold which is measured by a pressure transducer. Here a "computer" of sorts is used – an analog/digital converter which provides a digital signal to the electronic modules. Engine speed, read at the flywheel by a pick-up, also sends input to the module. Inputs are also provided to identify top-dead center locations, and all this is correlated so a perfectly timed spark can be sent to each cylinder at the right instant.

Mike Sheehan of European Auto Restoration, Costa Mesa, California gave the individual look to this 308 GTS, including a new front spoiler, a one-piece grille (involving removal of the heavy U.S. front bumper) and the rear wheel flares (to cover wider wheels & rubber).

Frank Milne, owner of Harry Mann Chevrolet in Los Angeles, is a Ferrari connoisseur. His 308GTB wasn't quite the way he wanted it so he had his agency bodyman, Eric Ruffo, design a new front spoiler with oil cooler scoop, and install Daytona bucket seats.

Gary Bobileff, of Bobileff Sports Cars, San Diego, California, modified this 308GTS, lowering it, installing modular wheels, wider tires, rear wheel well flares, a roof spoiler and two very large diameter chromium exhausts. Bobileff specializes in individualizing Ferraris and Lamborghinis.

Gary Bobileff saw this GTB being improved with rear wheel flares, wider tires on modular wheels, a deep front spoiler and full width grille.

The Improved "i" Models

Not long after the switch to fuel injection, Ferrari changed the clutch return spring linkage. The redesign of the clutch pedal spring anchor really improves the driveability of the GTB/GTS, and transforms the car from a baulky beast to one that can be driven easily in traffic. The new clutch has no free play, though, and takes some getting used to for those who are used to the stiff clutch with its 5mm of free play before engagement

Three things contribute to the driveability of the post 1980 models: the fuel injection with its smooth fuel delivery; the "soft" clutch; the TRX radials; and the oil pump on the gearbox, which simplifies shifting effort greatly. The only disappointments in this brightened picture are that these models are quieter – lacking the raucous induction roar of the carburetored cars – and they are slower, without the straining-at-the-leash feel common to the carburetored cars.

Fortunately, owners of carburetored cars can easily have the new clutch linkage fitted to their cars, but not many will want to go to the expense switching to the pump-pressurized gearbox just to further ease shifting effort.

Ironically, even though the fuel injection is responsible for the quantum leap in driveability in the 308, there are reports that some owners are buying intake manifolds that allow retrofitting of carburetors. Carburetors may be inefficient, and unsmooth in action compared to fuel injection, but they are more understood by those owners who like to do their own work, and this may become a growing trend – one that the Environmental Protection Agency in the U.S. would heartily disapprove of!

One of the minor styling changes in the "i" models was certain to cause conscientious owners heaps of trouble later on – and that was the switch from the admittedly cheap-looking vinyl on the ceiling and surrounds to a loose-woven natural-colored cloth. The cloth looked much more expensive than vinyl, but attracted dirt like a magnet, and – being loosely woven – offers no easy way to be cleansed of grime. The result is that the interior of '80-and-later 308's look older much faster, which must be making somebody in the upholstery business more wealthy, in anticipation of selling replacement kits.

The durability of the Ferrari leather is another bone of contention. On the author's 1979 GTS, the driver's seat bolster was cracked and worn at 12,000 miles, while on a 1982 Mondial 8, the upholstery was severely cracked with even less mileage. It may be the same Connolly leather, as furnished in a Rolls-Royce, but somehow the leather there seems to last longer. This lack of durability is what leads many Ferrari owners to buy sheepskin or cloth covers, or simply replacing the seats entirely with aftermarket units by Recarco or Scheel.

Before one gets the impression that all the styling updates are downhill in the "i" models, one improvement was changing the material in the wheels from the all-too-easily chipped magnesium to aluminum.

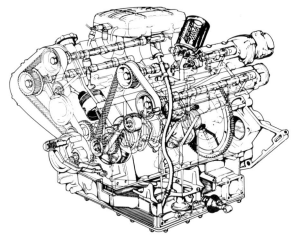

The fuel-injected 308 is basically the same engine as the carburetored one. The fuel injection was necessary to meet U.S. emissions standards, not added for more performance.

The Silver-Haired Fox and The Mystery Lady

It makes a most unlikely rally car, but yet a Frenchman, Jean-Claude Andruet, has made the 308GTB one of the most competitive sports cars in European rallying. He is a Ferrari enthusiast first, and that's what makes him choose a Ferrari to rally instead of an Opel Ascona 400, Audi Quattro or Renault Turbo, which are to the fore in Europe.

Andruet goes back more than a dozen years in racing, having driven rally cars (Stratos, Renault A110, R8 Gordini, Alfetta, Fiat Abarth 131) single-seaters (Formula 3 Alpine) and endurance racers (Ferrari Daytona, Gp. 4 Porsche, Ferrari BB512). He is one of the handful of drivers who has proven that a rallyist can also do well in road-racing (though in road-racing he has not enjoyed as many outright wins as in rallying), but he *has* succeeded in his ultimate ambition—driving Ferraris at Le Mans. The Ferraris are provided by Pozzi, the French Ferrari distributor. It would be better if they were provided by the works, but, alas, Maranello does not support any racers other than their own Formula One team.

His 308 GTB is a well-thrashed fiberglass (the French call it polyester, which makes it sound like a leisure suit) car with the engine juiced up to 310 bhp at 8000 rpm (basically Group 4 spec.) His own engine man, Michelot, replaced the carburetors with a Kugelfischer mechanical injection set-up, and the cams and pistons were also changed.

The brakes are 4-piston Lockheed calipers on wider, larger diameter discs. The car uses two oil coolers, and one water radiator with, surprisingly, only one electric fan.

The shocks are by Monroe and the wheels the same yellow Campagnolos used on Lancia Stratos rally cars—measuring 8″ × 15″ in front and 12″ × 15″ in the rear.

The entire stock dashboard was ripped out and replaced by a flat unit with a 10,000-rpm tach (redlined at 9500!), no speedometer, and the standard gauges re-installed in a straight row, joined by four push-pull switches for the road lamps.

Andruet switches final drives for different events, but with his long-course gears, he has reached 271 kmh at 8000 rpm (169.375 mph).

The most intriguing thing about Andruet's 308 effort—at this writing going into its second year of competition—is his beautiful navigator, a woman who insists on being identified only by the name "Biche" which is *not* what you think it is but, in a French dictionary, translates to "young woman." Pseudonyms were fairly common in European racing where young men were scared of losing the family inheritance should dad find out about their exciting new hobby.

But when the *non de plume* is a beautiful woman, it makes things that much more interesting. . . .

A limited slip ZF differential is used, set at roughly 80. The GTB, set up Andruet's way, is extremely difficult to drive because it takes sheer muscle to steer and brake, especially when compared to the Audi Quattro or Lancia Stratos. But Andruet wants to be identified with Ferrari, so he suffers the inconveniences to win the factory's attention (and, hopefully, eventual support!) (L'Autombobile)

The so-called GTRi convertible ("R" for roadster) is the brainchild of Ekkehard Zimmermann—a former Ford of Germany designer—whose company, DP Design, also builds the bodies for the incredibly fast Kremer Porsches.

The Germans were onto turbocharging the 308 well before the factory. The Koenig unit looks fancy, and is, enabling the 308 to get up above the 150 mph cruising speed that Germans feel a real sports car should have.

Zender Ferrari, based in Germany, not only makes up new spoilers, but even wind-tunnel tests them! These cars also have their rocker panel moldings and special rear valance panel. (Wolfgang Rempath/Sportfahrer)

One of the first Americans to take up the 308 as The Car to develop was Joe Alphabet, of Alpha Design Engineering, in Huntington Beach, California. Alphabet developed his own front spoiler, which has air intake holes for brake cooling, his own Boxer-type rear roof spoiler, a custom grille to give a flush-fit Boxer-type look (prancing horse centerpiece is extra) and a set of front and rear European-type bumpers made of lightweight fiberglass. Maybe the latter won't be that much protection in an accident, but anything to take weight off the heavier American version is appreciated by the hard-core enthusiast.

Perhaps the most significant styling change Alphabet made to his 308 test car was the refinishing of the targa top to a smooth surface painted body color, and the removal of the side louvers covering the rear 3/4 windows, which he felt gave the GTS too much of a "plastic look." Other styling changes included pulling out the rear 3/4 panels almost one inch per side, which deepened the side scoops, flaring the rear fenders, and designing a new rear undertray which accommodates the twin barrels of the Alphabet-designed exhaust.

The wheels are Gotti modular units, 8″ × 16″ in front, 9″ × 16″ in the rear, carrying Pirelli P7's, sized 225/50 in front and 265/50 in the rear. It took considerable wheelwell work to make this wide rubber fit.

Luis Dallazen of Luis Ferraria Ferrari of Costa Mesa, California handled the engine work, porting the heads, re-grinding the cams and adding 10.2:1 pistons. The 1978 GTS now looks and acts like something closer to a race car than a street car, yet is still fully street driveable.

To love it is to change it . . .

Some Ferrari afficionados simply can't abide by Ferrari's snail-like pace in development of new features for their production cars (when it comes to *race* cars, the firm is a *whole* lot quicker) and in America, turbocharging the 308 was a popular modification at least two years before Ferrari tried it in a production car.

The Germans, meanwhile, decided that a Targa top didn't provide enough sunshine and one German dealer, called Auto Becker, in Dusseldorf, has sold several 308 GTS models converted to *full* convertibles with canvas soft tops. Ferrari hasn't made any statement as to what *they* think of this conversion, though they no doubt are a bit put out that someone beat them to it!

One of the favorite modifications of 308 GTB and GTS owners is to switch from the easily-chipped magnesium wheels to modular types, with detachable wheel rims so that different size tires can be tried. The most popular modular rim has been BBS from Germany and many other types, including steel wire wheels, have been tried. Ferrari, predictably, disapproves of wheel and tire changing when their suspension has been set up to work with a certain offset wheel and tire brand. But those enthusiasts in search of certain goals cannot wait for "official" alternatives and the 308 shows signs of becoming a popular weekend time-trials car like the 246 Dino before it. And, because of its stunning shape, it also is becoming a favorite of the Concours d'Elegance set, who will doubtless refinish the car to standards far beyond what Ferrari and Pininfarina ever dreamed of.

If you want to go fast, you need bigger tires. If you want bigger tires, you need bigger wheels. If you want bigger wheels, you need bigger fender flares. If you . . . well, you get the idea. Shot at Riverside California in 1981.

While this custom wheel well flare smooths the aerodynamics of the 308 it also becomes a target for stones. Possibly, were Ferrari to adopt this modification, they would add a toughened cover as Porsche did on the 930 Turbo.

The "Gruppe 5" look comes to the street? The British owner of this GTB wanted wider wheels and tires on the back but didn't want to flare the wheelwells. So he widened the whole back of the car! He also added a Group 7-style wing.

The Mondial 8 is conservative, a more muted echo of the 308 and Boxer styling themes. (K. Oblinger)

The Mondial 8 was praised by European road testers but they weren't quite as enthusiastic about it as they had been about the GTB/GTS. (K. Oblinger)

In the back a small luggage compartment with factory-supplied tool kit and the engine are revealed. The large air intake scoops were necessary because of legislation in Germany (K. Oblinger).

The Open Air Project

Apparently, the spyder design does not provide enough fresh air to please all tastes, and in Germany, a private party was the first to create a full convertible out of the 308GTS, using a very long engine cover strongly resembling that in the one-off 1966 DeTomaso Mangusta Spyder designed by Giorgetto Giugiaro for Ghia. The convertible top itself is supported in the rear by an electrically or hydraulically-retractible chrome tube which looks at first like it could function as a roll bar, but actually is intended primarily to provide roof support when the convertible soft top is up.

The actual shape of the convertible top is skimpy in the extreme, which in a way is understandable since anyone who wants to spend the $20,000-or-so in conversion costs is planning on having the top down most of the time. The top is not designed for how it will look erected but only for how it will look when the top is down!

Apparently, there is no way for a conversion artist to patent his convertible top design and, soon after the first fully convertible 308 appeared in West Germany in 1980, conversion artists on both sides of the Atlantic began thinking of how they could hack away at 308 GTS models to create the same design. (It must have been felt that the GTS is a better candidate for conversion than the GTB because its frame is already beefed to counteract the increased structural loads imposed by the targa top).

Big Willi and the Street Racers

The way Ferraris come out of Maranello simply didn't meet the needs of German *Ferraristi*, who probably travel faster on a daily basis in their Ferraris than owners anywhere in the world.

Willi Koenig, of Munich, a Ferrari parts dealer and service mechanic, developed a series of modifications which aerodynamically prepare the car for 150-mph cruising, and various devices to allow the fitting of wider wheels and tires than Ferrari feels necessary.

One Koenig package for the GTB/GTS includes a front spoiler, flared fender wells, "step-in side boarders" (which look like running boards), front wheels measuring 7.5" or 8" wide, rear wheels measuring 9" or 11" wide, and Pirelli P7 tires, sized 225/50VR–15 in front and 285/40 or 285/50–VR15 in the rear. If you bring your car to Munich to have all this fitted, including the modification of the shocks and springs, the complete price as of mid-1981 was DM 15,310 or $7000 in U.S. dollars.

Koenig also offers mechanical improvements, such as a dual exhaust, a heavy-duty clutch, heavy-duty springs and shocks, a 280bhp engine (that's DM 17,000 alone!) or a turbo-kit to install on your present engine, which was priced in 1981 at DM 16,000.

How does Koenig get 280bhp out of a carburetored 308? By changing the cam, valve springs, pistons and carburetors. Beyond that, he isn't too specific.

Is there much demand for Willy's street racers? *Ja.* As of mid-'82, he had transformed at least 50 Ferraris into Koenig Specials and his influence has even spread to America.

Although the Koenig Specials look a bit "boy-racer", the aerodynamic mods such as the deeper front spoiler and Can-Am style tail wing are needed for the 1/3rd increase in power he says his turbo kit delivers.

The most dubious part of the Koenig kit is the "side boarders," but Koenig claims he tests his cars at speed, and they do apparently help to stabilize the car. We hope and pray Pininfarina never adopts them!

Another German firm that offers products for the 308 is Zender, based in Mulheim-Karlich. Hans-Alber Zender actually has developed front and rear spoilers for dozens of cars, claiming to refine them in a wind tunnel. Optional on many of the front spoilers are brake hoses to cool the front discs.

Among the bits they offer for the 308 are a front spoiler, a rear deck spoiler, a "ledge" for the body sides (Americans would call it a running board) and a re-shaped rear lower body panel which is beveled outward as on a Lotus Turbo Esprit.

They also offer alloy wheels which are 7" × 16" in front and 8" × 16" in the rear so they can hold very wide Pirelli P7's, sized 205/55–16 in front and 225/50–16 in the rear, or Goodyear NCT's.

Zender also offers a quad-exhaust system which adds at least 20 horsepower.

For the interior, Zender offers a console that attaches to the dashboard to the right of the instrument binnacle, thus allowing re-location of the guages and radio which were formerly in fairly inaccesable locations.

Americans might be a little surprised at the prices for many of these items – such as $700 for the rear spoiler – but no doubt the "plastic pirates" in the U.S. will be "splashing" copies – a practice common in the bolt-on accessory field.

Except for the Germans like Koenig, only one American firm at press time has done work in the suspension department. Lance Nist, of Pantera Specialists in Santa Ana, California, came up with larger-diameter sway bars in 1982, which feature Heim joints on the ends, which have less compliance than the stock units. The rubber bushings in his track-ready cars are replaced with plastic bushings that have less compliance.

*MOTOR's Rex Greenslade at the wheel
of a British-market model.*

This 308 is one of several converted by DP in Germany to a full convertible.

The Mondial 8 depended for its acceptance on many old Pininfarina design characteristics.

CHAPTER FOUR

Mondial 8

It was raining as the driver reached the crest of the grade. Far below him, he could see a village, or was it the St. Bernard hospice?

He slipped into third as he started down the mountain. One turn connected to another in a kind of fluidic movement. He had the rhythm and the engine and gearbox were co-operating, reacting perfectly to his every movement, simpatico.

Later, in the city, the three businessmen he entertained gave the car little notice. It was small, and Italian – that was all they knew. He was almost relieved when he dropped them off at the airport and once again turned alone toward the alps, their crests gleaming in the sun. The engine began to sing again as he picked up speed. It was singing the song of Ferrari. . . .

When the GT/4 was phased out in 1980, there were no outcries of protest – no crowds chanting at Maranello's gates. After all, Ferrari enthusiasts had the much more attractive GTB and GTS to take its place.

And, in countries outside the U.S., there was still the 400 model available if you wanted 2-plus-2 seating in a Ferrari. But the 400 was not sold in the U.S. by the official distributor (though illegal models continue to be imported and converted to U.S. specifications) and Ferrari sought to replace the "hole" in their marketing structure with a long wheelbase Pininfarina design more in keeping with the styling theme of the GTB/GTS.

Whether the impetus for the Mondial first came from Pininfarina, Ferrari's usual body designer, or from Ferrari, is unknown. This writer suspects it was Ferrari first asking Pininfarina to design a car around a certain-size package, this conjecture based on the fact that, when Pininfarina designs the car on *their* volition, there is usually a show car done by them first, such as in the case of the flat-12-powered front-engined "Pinin".

There is not only a need for extra seating capacity beyond two seats in other countries, but, indeed, the presence of two other seats – whether they are ever used or not – sometimes presents tax advantages in that the car is then judged a sedan. (In Japan, the Mazda RX-7, for instance has two small jump seats in the back, it being against the law there to produce a car which selfishly only has two seats in such an overcrowded country).

Thus the Mondial 8 was created first seen by the world at the Geneva Auto salon of 1980. One might correctly think of this car's lineage as the Bertone-bodied GT4 "re-interpreted" as a Pininfarina design. True, the design house headed by Sergio Pininfarina is more (in the eyes of Ferrari purists) *qualified* to design a Ferrari's shape, but the fact that the Mondial 8 comes out 13.8" longer, 5" higher, 3" wider, and 350 lbs. heavier than the Pininfarina-designed GTB doesn't sound like there was any concerted effort to preserve the performance character of the earlier car as the highest priority (an assumption one would automatically make with Ferrari, for what are Ferraris *for*?). Instead, the Mondial 8 was intended to be a 2-plus-2 in which the "plus-2" part could actually be sat in, by adults, in contrast to the 308 GT4, where the back two seats were actually more cosmetic than utilitarian.

The Mondial 8 insured its acceptance by the Pininfarina-oriented Ferrari contingent by squeezing as many of the characteristics of the previous Pininfarina-designed Ferraris into its design as possible – Boxer-style hood vents, 400 door handles, 308 GTB/GTS front spoiler and roofline, (even down to the "tunnel-back" or "sugar-scoop" rear roofline which allows a fastback side profile with a vertical rear window). Yet there are some curious features which jar the sensibilities of those whose tastes were honed on earlier Pininfarina-designed Ferraris. For instance, the huge glued-on "grate" covering the side

On a bright day, you would definitely have to wear sunglasses with this incredibly bright interior

This rhd (right-hand drive) British 308GTB has the full Koenig treatment – flares, rocker mouldings, rear wing, wide wheels, low profile tires.

This California-based 308 has its own "look" – rear flares, wide wheels & tires, and flat black blunderbuss-style exhausts. Track is Riverside, at a Ferrari Owner's Club event.

The 328 has simpler lines than the 308 because of the body-coloured rear bumper. European models like this don't have rear side marker light.

air intake scoops seems unnecessarily large and grotesque (when none had been needed to cover the air intakes on the flanks of the previous 246 series, or the Pininfarina 308 GTB/GTS). But, reportedly, some sort of cover was needed for the hole because of legislation in Germany which required all such intake holes to have a protective grate (who was supposed to be sticking their arm into intake holes can't be imagined but the law's the law!).

Another offense to the eye is the heavy emphasis put on bumper protection. It used to be that European models always had smaller bumpers than the American ones and that the bumpers "dominated" less of the overall look

The first Mondial 8's had the side grate painted black. When the enthusiast media proved unenthusiastic about this detail, Ferrari painted the grate body colour, but to date, the press hasn't "warmed up" to the car like they previously did to the GTB/GTS models.

One of the most controversial aspects of the Mondial 8 design is the leading edge of the sail panels, which is flat black.

of the car. But with the Mondial, even the European model looks just as "heavy with bumper" as the U.S. version.

A final aesthetic nitpick concerns the wheels. These are the 180 TR × 390 wheels designed previously for those GTB/GTS models carrying Michelin 240/55 VR 390 TRX tires, and have the same outward-projecting center spider that runs contrary in design tradition to all racing wheels, which for generations, have had deeply *inset* centers.

Mechanically, the Mondial 8 was virtually identical to the 308 GTB/GTS series except for a modification in the hubs to reduce kingpin offset – and thus reduce the sharp steering "kickbacks" encountered when you hit bumps. Taking a cue from Mercedes, the front suspension's upper wishbone mountings were angled to give some anti-dive when braking.

Ferrari touted the Mondial's biggest engineering change as the fact that the engine/transmission package was all contained in a removable subframe. Nothing new, really, since Maserati had the same thing in the Bora back in 1973, but, still, one ought to applaud *any* attempt to make servicing easier.

The Mondial 8 engine started out virtually identical to the "i" version of the 308 GTB/GTS, using Marelli Digiplex electronic ignition and Bosch K-Jetronic fuel injection. *Motor* magazine's Rex Greenslade, in his Dec., 1981 driving impression of a Mondial 8, first lamented the loss of horsepower for the injected engine (which he said produced 205 bhp at 6600 rpm in the U.S. version and 214 in the European version) compared to the carburetored GT4 version (which he quotes as producing 255 bhp at 7600 rpm) but then admits that "it may well be that in 1975 – when quoted figures weren't watched so closely by the authorities – that the 255 was a little more generous than it should have been". Greenslade, then, was acknowledging what sharp-eyed readers knew all along – that car magazine editors – particularly in the flush of a first acquaintance with a new performance car – are all too likely to swallow improbable manufacturer-supplied figures whole. Thus was the furor created earlier over the manufacturer's "190-mph" top speed claim for the

365 Boxer, a claim only disproved some three years *after* the car's introduction when the staff of a British car magazine found they couldn't get anywhere close to that figure.

The result of putting an essentially weaker (than the GT4's) engine in a heavier car (than the GT4) was a slower car, even though its numerically higher final drive . . . 4.063 compared to 3.71 on the GTB/GTS should make it faster accelerating. The GT4, after all, had been called "shatteringly quick" in *Motor's* January, 1975 road test. Indeed, one cannot help but marvel at how much faster *Motor's* test car was than the GT4's tested by American magazines, as shown by the published results. One explanation might be simply that British road testers feel more of a responsibility to their readers, to the point where they wring the utmost performance out of a given test car – regardless of the manufacturer's recommended redline – more so than American road testers. If the engine blows up from overstrain – so be it!

Driving the Mondial

Even though the Mondial has an oil pump added to the gearbox to pressurize it that the 2-seaters didn't have, *Motor's* Rex Greenslade found that it had the same fault as the GTB/GTS gearbox – an unwillingness to shift when cold. Greenslade termed second gear being "well nigh unobtainable" when the gearbox is cold, but, fortunately, reported it loosens up in a few miles. Ferrari also claims the pump reduces gear wear, quietens down the gearbox and keeps temperatures even throughout it. The driver doesn't know all this – all he knows is that, once it's warm, it shifts like the proverbial hot-knife-through-butter, or much better than the baulky shifter in the pre-i-series GTB/GTS models or GT4.

Just as in the 308 GTB/GTS, although the Mondial's steering feels impossibly heavy at parking speeds, and seems to be a strong understeerer in tight corners, the car lightens up at faster speeds. In Greenslade's words: "it comes alive with feel – it almost seems as if the car can defy the laws of motion, so great is the lateral acceleration that can be developed".

The club racer has road lamps affixed 288GTO-style at the grille cavity ends.

Here's a 308 fitted out for serious club racing, with a 208-Turbo-style NACA duct, flares all around, a higher tail.

Same club racer, this view emphasizing the very wide wheels and racing tires.

The Mondial and the 328: contrast in style.

In contrast to several earlier mid-engine cars (the most infamous of which was the Mangusta), the Mondial did not jump into that wicked condition known as "trailing throttle oversteer" when he lifted the throttle or was forced to brake in mid-corner.

Motor's road tester praised the ride quality of the Mondial, which he termed: "firm and jiggly at low speed, though never uncomfortable as any vertical jarring has been cunningly removed by subtle tuning of the dampers. At speed, over all surfaces, the ride smooths out to become more than acceptable – on motorway and smooth A-roads it almost qualifies for the magic carpet class". This writer – based on 14,000 miles in a 308 GTS – wouldn't go *that* far, feeling a Porsche 911SC has a better ride over a variety of surfaces, as does the Lotus Esprit. But the Porsche has potentially violent oversteer lurking in the wings at the limit of adhesion and Lotus construction borders on "flimsy" compared to Ferrari's so, considering its heavy weight, its ride and handling are quite comparable with its would-be competitors from Stuttgart and Hethel.

Ferrari has always lagged far behind its German competitors in "creature comforts" – their philosophy seeming to be: "You adapt to the car, the car doesn't adapt to you". Where Porsche was offering electrically-adjustable seats and many other "gadgets" as options, the interiors of Ferraris remained almost spartan (indeed, it is the only car in this writer's experience that for several years came without a factory radio). There has been some small "bending" of this philosophy with the Mondial, the steering wheel being made adjustable up and down an inch or two. But the length to which the clutch pedal must be depressed still prevented short drivers (under 5 ft.) from ever driving the car. In perhaps a leap too far forward into the gadget ("Did we really need this?") realm, the Mondial has push-button solonoid releases for the bonnet/engine/boot lids. The question is: "When the battery is dead, can you still open them?". The answer is: Yes, and there are manual over-rider's for each button.

The air conditioning system in the 308 GTB/GTS was always on the bare edge of being adequate, partly due to the placement of the three dash-top vents far forward on the center of the dashboard where they could do little more than cool the windscreen. The Mondial has the aforesaid vents plus a vent on each side of the dashboard to better circulate the air. But the heater is still very slow to warm up, and *Motor's* Rex Greenslade complained that the heating and air conditioning controls – and even the radio face – are located so far back on the console that the driver can't see them. (Not so on the American version, which has the air conditioning controls in an easy-to-reach box under the dashboard).

The gauges in the Mondial 8 are still Veglia-Borletti white-on-black circular units, but they have a new type face on the labels and numbers and are not only easier to read but better-illuminated at night. Unfortunately, the upper brow of the rectangular instrument housing protrudes outward a little too far, cutting off the tops of the two main gauges from the driver's view. One of the biggest improvements from the GTB/GTS gauges is the fuel gauge, whose needle no longer swings wildly from side-to-side as the fuel moves about during cornering.

There is also a digital clock which reads out time in both military (European) fashion and in U.S./English fashion and has an elapsed time mode like a stopwatch. But this too is located high on the dashboard, just under the overhanging brow, and it takes a contortion by the driver to read it.

One really odd departure from past Ferrari practice is the moving of the odometer and trip odometer out of the mph/kp/h gauge and onto a separate part of the dashboard where it resembles an hour meter on a piece of stationary industrial machinery. It may be easier to service now that it is separately located but somehow it now seems *too* prominent for this writer's tastes.

Rex Greenslade implied the electronic check control display was a gimmick intended to make the Mondial "modern". As you turn on the ignition, it indicates any failures in the brakelights, headlights, or if there is a lid improperly closed. It also monitors the levels of engine oil, transmission oil, screenwasher fluid and air conditioning fluid. A clue to lack of temperament in this engine, perhaps, is a "service due" light that comes on 3000 miles after the last service.

Road & Track's testers also found the warning light console of limited value: "Attractive though it is," they wrote in their November, 1981 test, "the check panel is located well out of normal sightlines, its LEDs are barely visible in daylight and these tend to minimize its usefulness". Obviously, while embracing modern technology, Ferrari had failed to note what watch-makers had discovered 10 years earlier – that liquid-crystal displays are superior to LED's because they can still be read in daylight.

Even though one would assume that, with the increased emphasis on seating four people in the Mondial over the GT4, there would be more luggage room, such was not the case. The carpeted luggage compartment – at 6.5 cubic feet – was less than in the GT4's 6.7, which means those extra two people had better not pack any luggage.

In the U.S. version – which has catalytic convertors under the luggage bin – the luggage bin gets *very* warm on even a short 1-hour trip. The results can be devastating should one attempt to stow film or perishables in this area. Alas – some mid-engine cars might have averted this problem through careful exhaust routing in the late 60's – but not now when catalytic convertors are mandatory. If you're wondering what soft luggage was invented for, it's cars like the 308 which cannot accommodate conventionally-shaped "hard" suitcases.

And even though the increase in wheelbase would lend one to assume that the rear seats are actually "sitable," *Road & Track* felt that the 32.5" of headroom made the rear seats only fit for small children though they did concede "there's a bit more leg room than in the GT4 and though you might find it acceptable to splay your knees around the front seatback, but you can only slouch so much".

The seats of the Mondial 8 are shaped differently than those in the GTB/GTS. They seem to have more cushioning, but to this author, seemed more slippery—perhaps because they are not so "deep-dish."

The Mondial 8 presents a rather sedate image compared to the GTB/GTS, especially when it is painted a dark color. This is a European model, one of several dozens imported to the U.S. prior to Ferrari North America's "official" importation of the car.

erformance

Road & Track's test crew confessed open disppointment in the Mondial's performance. heir 0–60 mph time of 9.4 seconds and uarter-mile of 17.1 seconds at 83 mph they ɔund "less than scintillating", since these mes were slower than their GTSi test car. hey felt that the added 390 lbs. was the culrit. "Not only did the engine feel somewhat trained at wide open throttle", they wrote in Jovember, 1981 "but even more disappointग, it was missing the low-and-mid-range reponsiveness we've come to enjoy from other uel-injected Ferrari V8's. Succinctly, the Monial made all the right sounds, but it just didn't ɔ".

The Italian magazine, *Auto Capital*, testeɑ a Mondial 8 in 1982 and compared it many times to the old Bertone GT4. "It is a weaker car," they wrote. "In the 0–200 km/h run, it took 13.5 seconds longer to get to 200 km/h than did the old GT4." But the Mondial 8, with fuel injection as standard, was considerably more stingy on fuel, using 16 liters/100 km while the old 308 GT4 used 20 liters.

Road & Track's testers noticed that, since the Michelin tires are taller than those fitted to the 308 GTB/GTS, they also lengthen its stride "evidently to the detriment of its kick". They pointed out that, "in 5th gear at 60 mph, for example, the Mondial's tach shows 2900 rpm compared to the 308's 3200". While they didn't feel the top speed was hurt (they estimated 135 mph), they were somewhat embarrassed when they checked their records and found that the Porsche 924 Turbo, Alfa Romeo GTV-6 and Datsun 280ZX Turbo *all* proved to be faster to 90 mph than the Mondial.

Few U.S. magazine staffs test for lateral acceleration, which is expressed in terms of a side *g*-force reading. *Road & Track* does, by renting a test track with a circle painted on a flat surface and driving around said circle at a steady rate, obtaining the max *g* reading at a point just short of losing adhesion. With the Mondial, they recorded a reading of 0.812 *g* – the same as they recorded previously on their test GTB. This would be impressive were it not common knowledge that some much cheaper cars – like the $13,000 1982 Pontiac Firebird Trans-Am – can generate a 0.85 reading on the same skidpad. *Road & Track* also had an old Ferrari bugaboo pop up in their Mondial test – a momentary complete drop in oil pressure – something that had happened earlier with a 1977 308 coupe being tested for them by race driver Bob Bondurant. "There's a straightforward fix for it, though," they wrote, "involving removal of the oil pan and slight realignment of the oil pump's pickup; apparently, production tolerances are enough to cause this problem on some cars, but not others".

Motor, in their Dec. 1981 driving impression, wrote: "Enter a corner too quickly and lifting the throttle produces a mild tightening of the line – enough to scrub speed off without requiring a specific steering correction – and even if you're forced to brake in mid-corner, hard, the Mondial slows without an excessive change of attitude. This stability is one of the Mondial's fortes and the Ferrari engineers deserve the greatest compliment for managing to blend such good high speed stability (even at 120 mph on a bumpy country road with the wheels pounding up and down like pistons the Mondial feels rock-solid on line) with a lack of understeer and a neutrality in strong cornering."

Motor's staff did find, on damp leaves, excessive throttle could "make the tail step out of line very smartly indeed". They warned: "You have to be very quick and accurate applying opposite lock, though just the right amount of castor action is a considerable help".

Even though the Mondial lacks a high-technology braking system like the Mercedes ABS-system (which uses an on-board microcomputer to modulate braking pressure in order to prevent a skid with its subsequent loss of steering control). *Motor's* staff felt that the brakes "must be as good as that of any road car in the world today". They praised the progressive and positive action but only found fault with the handbrake, which in the right-drive test car was so close to the stereo speaker that each time they used the handbrake, they skinned their knuckles.

While the regular brakes work exceptionally well, the handbrake is one of those maddening types that folds down to be out of the way even when it is in the "on" position. This causes some consternation when the car won't move forward until the dash light tips you off that the brake is on. Then you have to lift the lever with a mighty heave and depress the release button, to be able to fold it flat in earnest. The Porsche 914 had the same cursed arrangement

One thing no road testers (upto the time of publishing this book) mentioned was the "forward control" feeling one gets in a Mondial 8. The feeling is much more akin to a modern GP car seating position than one gets in the GTB/GTS. The driver feels as if his legs are extending over the front axles. Even the view out the Mondial windscreen shows only a hint of hood, compared to the sensuous bulges in the hood of the GTB/GTS or even Boxer.

Whether one likes it or not depends on where you like to be when you initiate a turn. In the GTB/GTS, you feel like you're in the centre of the car, with an equal amount of car both ahead and behind you. In the Mondial 8, when you turn, you feel as if you're a lot further up front with the great mass of the car following you. You get used to it, but it's a different feel that some drivers may never acclimatize to.

The Mondial – in 2-valve form, and in U.S. specification – does nothing until you are going either 70 mph or above 6000 rpm. In other words, it not only has a very muted sound to the exhaust, it has very muted performance as well. When you finally can go down a winding country road at speed – say 6000 rpm in third – *then* it begins to feel like a Ferrari. But in city traffic, it could be almost any car as far as the sense of power-on-tap one gets. If the Mondial 8 sells any Ferraris, it is GTB's and GTS's because it makes them look like tigers.

It is difficult to imagine what goal Ferrari and Pininfarina had in mind when they designed the Mondial 8. If it was luxury, they fell far short of a 928. If it was performance, they even fell short of a 944 – a car which cost 1/3rd as much! If it was four seats, and a Ferrari engine, they already build that car – the 400 Automatic. How did Ferrari miss the mark by so wide a margin? It may be due to their isolationism – a legacy of the Old Man's philosophy of building it the way Ferrari wants to build it regardless of what others are doing. It could be a costly mistake for the firm.

Auto Capital's staff writers were philosophical about the Mondial:"Lovers of exotic sports cars and lovers of Ferrari naturally don't pay attention to the few things that the car lacks. Whether they can accept the fact that it is not as powerful (as the previous Ferraris), and has less bite, remains to be seen from sales. It is too early to make a prediction.''

What the introduction of the Mondial 8 *did* accomplish, in a nutshell, was to mark with a model change what had already been happening since the introduction of the GT4 308 back in 1975 – the moving of Ferrari into what you could call the ''turn-key'' class. That meant you just get into the car, turn the key, and go, as if the car were no more complex than a Buick. (The author is reminded of a visit to Maranello he made in April, 1982, where he saw an all-white BB 512 with an all-white interior at the factory, symbolizing that the BB 512 is now regarded by Ferrari as a car which will never suffer a messy breakdown or even be so impolite as to leak oil. With that color combination, it wouldn't *dare*!)

Ferrari is reportedly considering making a car even more luxurious than the present 400—the Pinin, which made its debut as a prototype in 1980 at Turin. The front end will likely be re-shaped and the 308's V8 may go under the hood instead of the Boxer's flat-12 since the V8 already has passed U.S. emissions standards. Its production may result in the 400 being phased out.

208 For Italians Only

The 208

Italy and France are energy-conscious countries. Accordingly, there are all sorts of contrivances on the part of the State to reduce the number of large-displacement cars on the road, and even though an American used to 5-liter V8's wouldn't think of the Ferrari's 3-liters as especially *large*, the Europeans think of 3 liters as positively *monstrous* in size, and discourage engines larger than two liters by 1) charging more on the autostrada toll roads for cars over 2-liters than for cars under 2-liters 2) charging a much greater tax upon purchase for a car over two liters than for those under that displacement.

Ferrari evidently thinks it is important politically to sell cars in Italy (DeTomaso doesn't, having sold only six of the 86 he produced a couple of years ago in Italy). Therefore, they devised a downsized-in-displacement 308 called a 208. It was available in Europe on all three body styles – the GT4, GTB and GTS.

The engine had a reduced bore – at 66.8 mm – but the same stroke as the 308 – 71 mm, and displaced 1991cc. The compression ratio was 9:1 and the horsepower rated in Italy at 170 at 7700 rpm compared to 255 for the 308. Although the compression ratio was the same as the 308, at 9:1, the carburetors were smaller – Weber 34 DCNF's rather than 40 DCNF's.

Presumably because of the lesser demands made on the chassis by the weaker engine, the 208 came with narrower tires – 195/70VR14 XDX instead of the 205/70VR14 Michelin X's normally fitted (until the TRX became the standard tire on the 308).

Like all European 308's, it only had one Marelli distributor.

Although the European 208 might get better mileage than the European 308 or American-specification 308, one can't help but conclude that – for anyone who lives outside a country where they tax displacement – the car would be undesirable compared to a 308 since it has one-third less engine but still has to haul around a car that's as heavy as the 308.

This author has heard of only one 208 converted to a 308 by its owner, but if the GTS model in particular begins to climb in price on the used car market worldwide, buying a used 208 GTS in Europe and converting it to a 308 GTS in one's native country might be thought of by more people as a way to have a lower cost open Ferrari. But the paperwork for the car – plus the engine plate, chassis i.d. numbers, etc., etc., will *still* say "208" so this course is recommended *only* if one is building the car for one's own use, not for resale where the charge of fraud could crop its ugly head if somewhere along the way 308 insignia was fitted to the car and the car represented and sold as an *original* 308.

The 208 Turbo

Ferrari took a tentative step into the "state-of-the-art" automotive world in April, 1982, when they introduced a turbocharged production model – the 208 Turbo – for only the Italian market at the bi-yearly Torino Auto Salon.

Why the Italian market only? Because the taxes for registering a three-liter car are at least 17% higher in Italy than for a two-liter. That's why the two-liter V8 had been available in the 308 since the introduction of the GT4. But the normally aspirated two-liter wasn't a very satisfactory performer when you consider it had the job of moving around the same number of kilograms of weight as the three-liter does.

The obvious solution was to follow Porsche again. Ferrari had already followed Porsche with the use of K-Jetronic fuel injection, and now it followed Porsche with the use of a turbocharger.

The turbo pumps the 208 up from its normal European 208 rating of 170 bhp (DIN) to 220 bhp (DIN) at 7000 rpm. The addition of the exhaust-driven turbocharger required a slightly different exhaust with the turbo drawing its power from a pipe connected to the transverse silencer.

Ferrari was forced to employ a single-turbo installation because the engine's transverse location makes only one side accessible, at least with all the street equipment installed. Somehow, in 1980, Italian racers Carlo Facetti and Martino Finotto managed to squeeze twin turbos into a GTB which they entered in the Daytona 24 Hour. After posting the fastest time in practice the 840 bhp (claimed!) car only completed six laps and then dropped out of the race.

Like other auto makers offering turbochargers, Ferrari also felt it necessary to put a rev limiter on the *turbolader* engine, if only because, in a turbo, the tach needle climbs upward so much more rapidly than in a normally-aspirated car. It was felt that the driver might not have time to "shut it down." In the 208 Turbo, the "cut-out" begins at 7800 rpm or when the pressure nears 10 psi.

The KKK (Kuhnle, Kopp and Kausch) compressor is the same type used on Ferrari's Formula One car, though not with the same capacity. The street turbo is called the K26 and is very similar to that used on the Porsche Turbo 930.

The 208 Turbo also introduced two functional body modifications to the V8 series that had previously been used in the Boxer – a transverse "wastegate"slot in the front hood to help exhaust hot air that had already passed through the radiator and a NACA-type flush-deck air scoop on each rocker panel.

In anticipation of the boost in pressure (which is cut out when it reaches 8.5 psi or 0.6 bar, measured metrically), Ferrari installed 7:1 compression ratio pistons in the 208 Turbo in place of the usual 8.8:1 pistons. These will also make it possible to burn unleaded gas when the turbo is offered in the U.S.

Another measure of the relatively unsophisticated design of the Ferrari Turbo is the lack of an intercooler, essentially yet another radiator used in addition to the normal water radiator and oil cooler. What the intercooler does is cool the compressed air that comes out of the turbocharger *before* it reaches the engine – cooler air being denser than warmer air and thus delivering more power. The Audi Quattro, Porsche 930 Turbo and even Renault Fuego use intercoolers as standard equipment but Ferrari either didn't have room for it or didn't think it necessary.

The transverse location of the 308 engine becomes an additional liability (servicing costs more because of it) in terms of its compatibility with a twin-turbo system. Maserati uses a twin turbo because they found that with two small turbos, there is less load on each one, which adds to the durability of the system. But then, the Maserati Biturbo V6 is mounted longitudinally, which makes a turbo on each side of the engine possible.

The 208 Turbo – with a top speed of 150 mph (242 km/h) is faster than the standard normally aspirated 208, but still slower than the Lotus Turbo (2174cc) or Porsche 930 Turbo (3299cc). But it's an irrelevant comparison because the 208 Turbo was developed for an under 2 liter engine, and also it is widely suspected of being just the "test bed" for the 308 Turbo desperately needed to revive the 308's failing reputation as a car that "looks faster than it is."

The 208 Turbo had its insignia in the standard place but the "turbo" lettering was so stylized that it was almost unreadable.

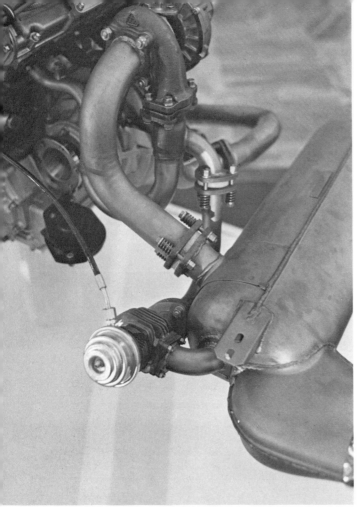

One of the interesting little tricks on the Ferrari 208 Turbo is the "expansion joints" on the tubing. The idea is that when the metal gets hot and expands, the little springs will accommodate expansion, where solid joints might lead to cracking and splitting of pipes.

The 208 Turbo, announced at the Torino Salon in 1982, had a deep front spoiler, a hood vent, a roof spoiler and NACA ducts. The Pininfarina label had to be moved to the rear fender because of the duct.

The 208 Turbo interior marked the introduction of a new cloth interior to the 2-seater body style. The seats had cream leather side trim, dark red piping and light brown wool "Zelna" cloth. A boost gauge replaced the clock, with a digital clock installed on the dash taking the place of the old circular clock.

The Return of the 208 Turbo

In 1986, the 208 Turbo was revised, this time bringing a little F1 technology into it, by adding an intercooler. According to Ferrari, the intercooled version pumped out 254 horses (DIN) compared to the 220 of the previous 2-liter 208 Turbo. More impressive was the one third increase in torque – from 24.5 Kgm for the non-intercooled car to 33.5 Kgm for the intercooled one.

In addition the intercooled car also produced its peak power and torque at least 500 rpm below the old engine, meaning you didn't have to wind it to the max to get max power.

As far as the speed capability, in their 208 Turbo intercooled press kit, issued in 1986, Ferrari claimed that the old 208 Turbo would go 0-to-100 km/h in 7.8 seconds while the new intercooled one would do the same job in 6.3 seconds. For a top speed, they listed the new one as capable of 206 km/h (128 mph) while the old one was listed as only being able to muster a 190 km/h (118.75 mph) top speed. Neither was very impressive to owners of 3-liter cars, who could top 263 km/h (164 mph) according to the same booklet.

But, in a comparison of speeds with the 3.2 liter non-turbo 328GTB, the 208 intercooled Turbo was a very close match in all else but top speed. After all, it had 127 hp/liter compared to the 328's 84.8 hp/liter.

How can you make a 308 stand out from the pack? Paint the bumpers body color like this one seen at the Ferrari Club of America Convention in 1987.

The 208GTB Turbo – offered mainly as an Italian-market model to get around the excessive taxes charged on cars over two liters – had a second generation model when the 328 came about, but it still has 2 liters, though 16% more power (254 hp.) than the 1st generation model. Torque was increased by 37%.

This Michelotto-modified 308 has a wing made by an American craftsman. Normally aspirated, it probably runs almost as fast as a 288GTo on a tight course.

CHAPTER FIVE

The 308 Quattrovalvole

The 308 Quattrovalvole

In 1983, Ferrari introduced a 32-valve version of the 308. Externally, except for cooling louvers on the front hood and the word "Quattrovalvole" on the rear valance panel, it looked just like the old 308.

The interior was only slightly changed — from a vinyl headliner, they went to a loose weave material that attracted dirt like a magnet.

The real news was the Type F105A V8. The displacement was the same, but the 32-valve heads were cast alluminum alloy mated to a new block with a redesigned combustion chamber. The head gasket was a better material. The valve guides were changed to tellurium copper-bronze for better expansion properties and the exhaust valves changed to solid ones of Nimonic alloy, seated in cast iron valve seats. The cylinder linings were changed to removable aluminum wet linings and the cylinder walls are Nikasil.

The compression ratio was raised from 8.8 to 1 in the European versions to 9.2 to 1. Unfortunately, due to the American requirement to run on unleaded fuel, the U.S.–spec. QV's had to stick with an 8.6 to 1 compression ratio. The European magazines listed the QV as having 230 hp. at 6800 rpm (up 25 hp) and 188 ft-lbs. of torque at 5500 rpm (up 7 ft-lbs.) The American distributor made the same claim for the American-spec. version.

The significant thing was not so much the increases in power and torque, but by the fact that the car was vastly improved in drivability — the torque present over a broader rev range — and you no longer had to "row" the gearbox to get it up to the rpm level where it would pull strongly.

Driving the 308

The QV version of the 308 was already two steps removed mechanically from the original

— it had fuel injection instead of carburetors, and twice as many valves as the original.

But the changes made in the rest of the car were so minimal as to be negligible, and road testers found many of the same old things to complain about as on the earlier 308's — a notchy shifter, a high interior noise level, a non-adjusting steering wheel and pedals that were too close together.

The handling of the QV was basically the same as the 308 — the general rule was "treat it right, and it'll treat you right". The tires were either the Michelin TRX 220/55R-390 radials on 165TR390 wheels or Goodyear NCT's, mounted on 7J x 16 wheels in front and 8J x 16 wheels in back. The Goodyears, unlike the Michelins, came in two different sizes front and rear, the fronts being 205/55VR-16's and the rears 225/50VR-16's.

Car & Driver's Pat Bedard, testing a 308GTS QV with Michelins, said: "As you approach the limit, the car understeers securely under power, but the lift-throttle characteristics are nasty: the tail comes right out, too far and too fast to be a handy course-correction aid." Bedard thought the wider Goodyears in the back would help, but at that time he hadn't driven the Goodyear equipped version.

The testers from Britain's *Motor* magazine weren't quite so pessimistic when they tested the Michelin-equipped version in 1983: "It is only in the wet that the 308 can be provoked into biting back, with both terminal plough-on understeer and fairly abrupt lift-off oversteer lying in wait for the unwary driver. In the dry, the Ferrari is supremely forgiving but at the same time very rewarding to drive hard and fast."

Motor also praised the 308QV's brakes, saying that, although they lacked anti-lock (then common on Mercedes), they worked progressively, and had strong stopping power with excellent feel and, most important, a total absence of fade — a flaw of some '60's Ferraris like the 275GTB.

The fuel consumption of a Ferrari is not that high on the list of priorities of buyers, who could buy anywhere from five to ten new economy cars for the same price of a single new Ferrari. But *Motor's* 19.6 mpg is worthy of note, though *Car & Driver's* 14 mpg is more realistic.

Creature Comforts

Ferraris may be expensive like Porsches or BMW's but the fundamental point to remember is that, with Ferraris, the driving comes first; everything else (like creature comforts) is secondary; almost unimportant.

That is why, coming from a car like a Porsche 928 or Mercedes 450SL to a Ferrari 308GTSi or GTBi is such a shock – so many of the controls and features are so rudimentary. The air conditioning, for instance, barely puts out cold air. It is sometimes necessary to have the air conditioning and heater on at the same time to get the interior temperature right.

Motor magazine also criticized the switchgear for being laid out haphazardly, with the biggest danger being in the headlight stalk which, if touched accidentally while driving, could plunge one into darkness.

The dashboard lighting was also stone-age; and at night the dashboard lights are annoyingly reflected in the windscreen. Both these faults are carried over from the 308 GTB and GTS.

It is no use to complain about comfort in a Ferrari, though, for, as England's *MotorSport* magazine wrote in March, 1983 "All such ergonomic grumbles fade away, however, once you turn the key and fire up the V8 into willing action".

Rust Protection

Ferrari was a typical Italian exotic automaker until the mid-'80's, in that they thought of their products as toys for the rich who would soon tire of them and trade them in on a newer (and hopefully faster) model. Hence, rust control was not a high priority. Indeed, Ferraris rusted just as fast as Maseratis or DeTomasos until 1983 when Ferrari began coating the steel with something called "Zincrox" that had a zinc content that resisted rust. The underside of the car was also coated with a plastic material. The rust-proofing program started on the 512BBi Boxer and slowly spread to other models.

Price

The Quattrovalvole was higher-priced than the previous 2-valve 308, with *Car & Driver's* test car being $59,500 for a GTS, up at least $14,000 from the price of a 2-valve carburetored 308GTS in 1979.

In England and on the Continent, the price went up as well, with *Motor's* 1983 308GTB QV coupe costing £27,128 including the huge Value Added Tax of over £3,000 and the £947 air conditioning option.

Unfortunately, the used car prices of 308GTBi and GTSi QV's continue to reflect the general downward trend of V8 Ferraris overall – that is to say, they depreciate rather than appreciate like most V-12 Ferraris. The price range for a used one can vary remarkably, as seen in the *Ferrari Market Letter* of 24 Jan. '87 where the "high" price for a 1982 308GTSi was listed as $43,000 and the "low" at $31,000. It all depends on condition, and mileage, as to how much value a given car retains.

The magic of Ferrari starts out pretty rudimentary. These are frames waiting to be taken into the factory and have their coachwork attached. Writing on the frame identifies them as 308 GTB chassis.

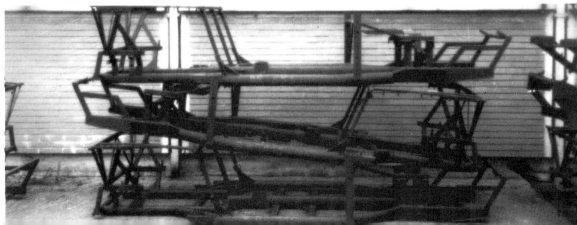

CHAPTER SIX

The Mondial Cabriolet

The European versions of the 3.2 Mondial have only a thin side marker in front rather than fore-and-aft markers as in the U.S.

The 3.2 Mondial

Ferrari and Pininfarina refused to drop the Mondial even when it was met with apathy by its intended buyers. To their credit, the cabriolet's introduction in October, 1983, turned the situation around. But the first cabriolets had top-engineering problems, and these were redesigned by September 1985 when a newer variation was introduced.

The next big change for the Mondial came when the 328GTB/GTS were introduced. It, too, received a minor "facelift" to give it some identity with the Testarossa.

The changes were similar to the 328's over the 308-body-coloured bumpers and flush-front turn signal lenses and fog lamps.

In an attempt to improve drivability at low speeds, the front tires were made smaller than the rears, and they were mounted on narrower wheels. If the brand was Michelin, the front tires were 220/55VR's while the rears were 240/55VR390's. If they were Goodyear Eagles, they were 205/55VR16's in front and 225/55VR16's in the rear.

The 3.2 Mondial was four inches shorter than the original model, which helped account for its 240 lb. lighter weight.

Inside, the instrument panel received minor changes, like red lettering on the Veglia dials instead of white, and an external temperature sensor for the air conditioning.

The Performance

In Europe, Ferrari quoted the top speed of the 3.2 Mondial at 250 kph, and magazine road testers were almost able to reach this. More importantly, it was at least matching the performance of the 308 GTBi and GTS QV's if not the 328, though still slower than the new 328GTB and GTS.

One significant change in the Mondial 3.2 was to fit narrower tires and wheels in the front than in the rear (220/55VR front; 390-290/55VR390 rear in European versions) in an

The dashboard of the 3.2 Mondial was redesigned with push-buttons to control many of the features. The center console has a lot of rocker switches and a light warning system. This one has a Blaupunkt radio, but there is no "official" Ferrari radio.

attempt to lighten up on the steering effort. Some feel that this added to the understeer characteristics, but only marginally.

Value

The Mondial 3.2 coupe may as well be a nonexistent model as far as the American-specification version is concerned, dealers preferring to sell the Cabriolet. The coupe would probably be a worse investment than the Cabriolet because of the low price of '83-'86 coupes on the used car market, most of them the slow and heavy 2-valve 308-powered versions.

The Mondial 3.2 coupe may legitimately have a market in Europe where the lack of sunshine (except on the Mediterranean and Aegean seas) makes a convertible useless, but in the U.S., it is the car without a market. The Cabrio allows one to enjoy the sun, and thus makes the concept viable. The 328GTB will still enjoy a market for those purists who dislike the lack of rigidity of an open car and still want a Ferrari but for whom the Testarossa is financially unreachable. The 412, incidentally, is not sold in the U.S.

The Mondial Cabriolet

When Ferrari had trouble selling the Mondial 8, they did what they had done years earlier with previous Ferrari models to make them more exciting – they cut the roof off.

The result, introduced in 1984 as the Mondial Cabriolet, was not aesthetically a *tour de force* but did at least satisfy the public's craving for a fully open Ferrari rather than a targa.

The Mondial Cabriolet came with the four valve head on the 3-liter V8.

The top was designed so that, when erected, it still had a fastback look by means of canvas "sail panels". From the back, it was less than pleasing, but with the top down, you had the effect of both abundant luxury and power.

The Mondial Cabriolet was called simply the Mondial Quattrovalvole and not the Mondial 8. It came with the same size wheels and tires front and rear – 240/55VR 390TRX Michelin radials.

The Mondial Cabriolet was a success saleswise, as it quickly sold out in America, and it also gave Ferrari time to finish up on the restyling of both the 308 and the Mondial.

Its biggest significance was that it brought new customers into the Ferrari fold, people who wanted luxury and performance but who originally came into the market because of the luxury and styling, and then came to appreciate the performance.

The Mondial Cabriolet was not really a four-seater in that four full-grown adults could take a long trip in it – it was more of a 2-plus-2, in that four adults could squeeze into it for a very short trip (with the rear seat passengers not at all comfortable). Of course, for children under 12, the rear seats were adequate. Seating-wise this car is more in the vein of the 365GTC/4 than the 400i.

One potentially un-nerving aspect of the Cabrio is that the driver and front passenger's seats are very forward in position, giving you the impression that the great bulk of the car is behind you. You don't feel as centrally-placed amidships as in the 308GTBi and 308GTSi and this impression could make some drivers uncomfortable.

The chief thing that the Mondial Cabriolet has going for it is exclusivity – when it was introduced, there weren't many ultra-luxury four-seater convertibles in the U.S. other than the Aston-Martin or the Rolls Royce Corniche.

It made a good "show-off" car, but not necessarily a practical long distance tourer for four, because even if you shoehorned in four passengers, the 308-sized luggage compartment could only hold overnight baggage for two.

The Mondial Cabriolet is primarily intended to be a pleasant tourer, not an all-out performance car. Hence, one can forgive its great weight – quoted at 3545 lbs. by *Road & Track* (but 3152 lbs by Ferrari), and its lower speed, which *Road & Track* quotes at 138 mph compared to the manufacturer's quote of 149.1 mph. But then again, R & T only ran it up to 6800 rpm where Ferrari's top end figure is calculated at the redline of 7700 rpm where it's "fully wound in top cog" as the British say.

The Cabriolet is less rigid than the coupe or GTS, so much that *Road & Track* commented on the flexing and shaking. In a slalom test, the same magazine's testers earned only a 0.80 later g-figure – lower than an '84 Corvette's .84 g-figure. But then, the Corvette has much wider tires, and is not a four-seater either.

In U.S.-spec. form, the Mondial Cabriolet could accelerate as well as the GTBi and GTSi – with a 0-60 mph time of 7.6 seconds.

The new car price for the Mondial Cabriolet at its U.S. introduction was $65,000 in 1985.

The used car price soon reflected depreciation, but the Ferrari North America organization guaranteed a high resale value in the U.S. by limiting the number of cabriolets imported.

Like the 328, the 3.2 Mondial has a more "filled-out" grille cavity to give the up-dated model more of a family resemblance to the Testarossa.

The front bonnet air outlet slats are more evident in this picture with this lighting. They increase the functionality of the cooling system by giving hot air that's passed through the radiator some place to go. This is a European model.

The rear of the 328 sticks closer to the 308GTB/GTS lines, except for the much neater slats hiding the exhaust system.

CHAPTER SEVEN

The 328 GTB/GTS

He was on the Grand Corniche, high above Monte Carlo. It was two days before the Grand Prix, and his uniform and helmet were beside him. He saw the exit for Monte Carlo, and threw a downshift, double-clutching to match revs. He cranked the wheel hard, came within an inch of the wall with the tail, flicked it into line, and accelerated, the 7000 rpm scream reverberating off the close-by mountain walls. Now he was on the Grand Prix course, the workers still putting up the fencing. In two days time, he would be driving another Ferrari here, one that could reach 200 mph . . .

The 328

In 1985, Ferrari announced a re-styled series of V8-powered cars, re-named as the 328, with the coupe being the 328GTB and the targa the 328GTS. The new name was keyed to the new enlarged displacement of 3185 cm, rounded off at 3.2 liters.

The "i" designation for injection was dropped, even though both the U.S.-spec. and models for the rest of the world had Bosch K-Jetronic fuel injection. By 1985, fuel injection wasn't rare enough any more to be used as a sales point. Ditto for the word "quattrovalvole" on the tail. It was useful when the 308 got it to distinguish it from the 2-valve but once the enthusiast was "educated" on this point, there was no longer a need to put the word on the back of the 328 as well.

If one looks at the power output of '60's Ferraris, it is remarkable how the horsepower figures climbed steadily, so that even street models like the 1971 365GTC/4 had more power than pure racers like the legendary 1963 250GTO. When the U.S. emissions laws looked like they would kill off performance in the 1980's, Ferrari responded to the challenge and the 328 has more power than its predecessor, yet is fully smog-legal. Ferrari met the challenge of the laws and overcame them with technology.

The Engine

The two intake valves in the 328 have a diameter of 29 mm each compared to the 42 mm diameter of the single intake valve used on the two-valve V8. The two exhaust valves on the 4-valve engine measure 26 mm across each while the single valve on the two-valve measured 36.8 mm. Thus, in a nutshell, you have the principal advantage of the 4-valve engine – more surface area in both the intakes and exhausts. Ferraris says the gas flow increase is 37% on the intakes and 41% on the exhausts, making the 4-valve V8 a much more efficient engine than the 2-valve in terms of what engineers call *"volumetric efficiency."*

The 328 engine is merely a larger version of the earlier 308 4-valve engine with a few minor changes. The bore and stroke were both increased – from 81 mm bore in the old model to 83 mm on the new model, and from 71 mm stroke on the old model to 73.6 mm stroke on the new one.

The total capacity change is from 2927 cc to 3185 cc. The compression ratio was changed from 8.6 to 1 to 9.2 to 1 on the U.S. spec. models. In Europe, it was changed from 9.2 to 9.8 to 1, improving the thermodynamic efficiency.

The torque took the biggest jump, from 188 to 213 ft-lbs. in the U.S. version, and this was where the car needed it most – it being a chore to "row" the gearbox lever to get up to speed in the 308.

Other engine modifications included higher profile cams on the inlet side with greater lift repositioned 12 mm spark plugs between the four valves in the chamber, new type holding rings between the cylinder liners and the block to reduce linear distortion under stress and a new Marelli Microplex ignition system in place of the older Digiplex. And even though the 308 rarely had cooling problems, the oil cooling

The interior of the 328 is still not far from its 308GTB/GTS origins, but has been up-dated somewhat. New are the interior door handles, the instrument cluster in the center of the dashboard and a few changes in switchgear.

radiator(s) in the 328 were made larger.

What the bigger motor did was bring the V8 model back into line with Ferrari's original objectives with the two-seater. They had originally met those objectives with the lightweight fiberglass-bodied dry-sump 1977 308GTB coupe but only about 200 were made before they switched to a heavier steel body and lost performance. The switch to fuel injection lost over 30 horses with the onset of the 1980's – a loss only partially made up for when the Quattrovalvole came into being.

Increasing the bore 22 mm and the stroke 2.6 mm brought the car closer to their "ideal" goal, which is around 250 hp. The European version is quoted as having as much as 270 hp DIN at 7000 rpm, though now all European cars have their power figured in *Kilowatts* with the 328's quoted as 198.7 kW at 7,000 rpm – a big jump from the 4-valve 308's 176.6 kW.

How much power a Ferrari engine is credited with depends on what specification you are quoting – U.S. or European. In Europe, Ferrari says that the European models have 270 hp (DIN) at 7000 rpm (or in the new way of measuring 198.7 kW for "Kilowatts"). In the U.S., Ferrari of North America quotes 260 hp.

(SAE) at 7,000 rpm. Ferrari North America never quoted the torque in their press release but *Road & Track* did in their May, 1987 test when they said it was 213 lb-ft at 5500 rpm compared to 188 lb-ft at the same rpm for the 308GTSi they tested back in 1983.

The maximum rpm quoted withe 3.2 liter engine was still 7700 rpm. Can a 308 or 328 go beyond this and live? The author once wound to 8,000 rpm on his 308 with no ill effect, but for longevity, it is best to adhere to the manufacturer's recommendations.

The Styling: a touch of Testarossa

The 328 styling was not revolutionary, but evolutionary, being basically an up-date of the 308 to make it look more like the more costly Testarossa in front.

This was achieved by giving it more of a "filled-out" look in front. Body colored bumpers front and rear also up-date the car, and at last the grille carried the traditional *"cavallino rampante"* (prancing horse).

The air slots behind the pop-up headlights were removed, giving the fenders a cleaner look.

The black vertical outside door handles of the 308 were changed to body-coloured flush units.

The 16" tall wheels still had a "star" pattern but a more sculptured appearance than before. Tires ranged from Goodyear NCT's in Europe, or Pirelli P7's, sized 205/55VR-16 in front on 7" x 16" wheels and wider 225/50VR16's in the rear on one-inch wider wheels. In America, Goodyear Eagle GT "Gatorbacks" were offered.

The 328 was, as was traditional, a car of few options, the only ones in the U.S. being metallic paint, a passenger side outside rear view mirror and a roof spoiler, while in Europe, air conditioning was still an option.

The 328 came with a longer "chin" spoiler than the American-spec. 308, but it wasn't as deep as the Euro.-spec. 308's chin spoiler had been. And it was finished in matte black and more "wrap-around" than the 308's original chin spoilers.

The 328 Interior

The interior of the 328 represented a more significant change than the "i" version did from the carburetored car. The 288GTO inspired the center-dash binnacle with three gauges. The emergency brake handle, which always had been in the way in the center console, was moved to the narrow space between the driver's bucket seat and the door sill.

And when it came to making it easy to close the doors, the 328 made it a whole lot easier by having inside door handles shaped like the hand-grips of a heavy machine gun. On the passenger side, the handle serves as a passenger "grab bar" to give him some security.

A door pocket was also added to the driver door inside door panel – any stowage space was appreciated.

Central door locking was added – other marques had enjoyed this long ago, but Ferrari had to wait until they could re-engineer them into

The tight packaging of the 328's engine transversely in the tubular chassis is seen here. Service operations are sometimes more expensive than front-engined V-12's because of the difficulty of access to the faulty parts.

The 328 engine looks almost identical to the 308 Quattrovalvoles, except for minor re-arrangements of some items. Wiring has become neater through the evolution of the breed.

the already existing shape.

The gauges were still Veglias but the lettering was changed to all red instead of white lettering as on the 308 and 308 "i" models.

The black-spoked steering wheel by Momo — wih its "thumb-notches", was retained from the 308QV.

On the center console, the slide controls used on the 308 and 308 "i" models were replaced by more modern switches. The center console also had a small storage compartment.

The Driving

The 328 is like a 308 2-valve would be if given a healthy shot of vitamins. The 0-to-60 mph time is almost a second faster — most magazine testers reporting around 5.5 seconds, and the top speed just clears 160 mph, in the European version. That speed could be beaten if one had properly-shaved tires as Britain's *Fast Lane* said in their May, 1987 road test of a 328GTSi: "Take off the tyre scrub which kept the tail yawing at 10 degrees or so for the duration, and you're into another five mph or so." (Goodyear, as a matter of fact, makes a tire in the U.S. for showroom-stock competitors that

comes pre-shaved for less tire squirm such as you get in a fully-treaded tire.)

Another way of judging the power of a car or the power available in different specification versions of the same model, is to compare their acceleration over the same distance or in the same time span.

Ferrari publicity released at the time of the 328GTB/GTS introduction, in 1985, in Europe said the European version would attain a 26 km/h top speed, and go from 0 to the end of one kilometer in 26.3 seconds. Ferrari of North America said the U.S.-spec. version would go 150 mph and do the standing kilometer in 27. seconds. So, in other words, they were saying the U.S.-spec. version was about one second slower than the European version. If so, there is no longer the vast difference that existed before between European 308's without catalytic converters, so that there is less reason now for any American to buy a "gray market" European-spec. Ferrari and bring it to the U.S for "Federalization."

Quotes about speed from car magazines are highly compromised by a myriad of factors including such objective ones as co-efficient of friction of the road surface; length of the straightaway, and quality of the fuel. Add t hat such imponderables as the skill of the driver, whether or not there was a co-driver, weight of test equipment, brand of tire and their inflation pressures, and whether the driver was willing to fudge figures so he could take a longer lunch hour!

Keeping all this inexactitude in mind, one can at least get some idea of the performance by comparing magazines results from different countries.

The driver in *MotorSport*, the British publication, reported on a 328GTB in their March, 1987 issue, and found that it went 0 to 60 mph in six seconds and reached 100 mph from a standing start in 14.7 seconds. Thus he beat the time quoted by Ferrari North America in 0-to-60 mph by a full 1.4 seconds!

He also quoted a top speed of 151 mph.

The respected American journal, *Road & Track*, reporting on a 328GTS in their May, 1986 issue, matched the British tester with a 0-60 mph time of 6 seconds and a top speed of 149 mph.

The higher top speed was not only due to the increased size of the engine but the change of the final drive ratio from 4.06 to 1 to 3.823 to 1. *Road & Track* also quoted a curb weight for the 1986 328GTS of 3170 lbs. vs. 3250 lbs. for the 1983 308GTSi, which means that somewhere Ferrari cut out 80 lbs., good for probably one or two mph.

The 328 steering is still heavily "weighted" at lower speeds like the 308, and becomes easier as you increase speed, feeling ideal at about 70 mph cruising speed. *Road & Track*, the American magazine which has built a cult around Ferraris, nevertheless complained about the 328's steering in their May, 1986 report, saying: "the response is a bit slower than we would like and the car feels like it needs more caster built in because the steering doesn't center itself easily." They would have preferred the wheel to be quicker in its "recovery" after a turn. They also disliked the angle of the steering wheel, which made it difficult for them to do a fast time on the slalom test.

The 328 continues the 308 virtue of being unaffected by hot temperatures or traffic jams – never overheating.

The 328 also starts readily – this being the

The roof spoiler on this British-market 328GTS is body color, rather than black as on most 328's. This change may have been done by the British distributor.

advantage of the fuel injection over the old 308's carburetors. And it no longer revs high at idle like the first 1980-model injected 308's did.

But it is still difficult to engage both first and second gears when the gearbox is cold. In fact, it is a good idea to double clutch on all upshifts and downshifts while the car is still warming up. Another idea this driver used on his 308GTS was to start out in first from a traffic light and skip second gear entirely, going straight to third until the gearbox oil is warm.

Ride quality is something you expect in a car that cost $50,000 but it is difficult to achieve the ambience, say, of a BMW sedan when you ask the 328 to be capable of high-g cornering, and yet be styled similar to a racing car.

Autoweek's road testers were certainly dissatisfied in March, 1986 with their 328GTS' ride when they said "the suspension is nearly solid and the shock is transmitted as a very severe jar to the occupants."

The noise level is, of course, high. The enthusiast who buys a Ferrari presumably will enjoy this noise, but as Ferrari does depend on this concept more than other auto-makers, such as BMW with their 535i, a fast car where the engine is much less intrusive.

The road tester at Britain's *MotorSport* magazine, reporting on a 328GTB in their March 1987 issue, found that the 328 exhibited a bit of body roll in cornering, but he didn't mind, saying it was "sufficient to impart a welcome degree of 'feel' to the driver."

Driver positioning is a delicately-discussed matter, for Italians dislike references to the long-armed short-legged driver that must be used as their model for seat positioning. *Autoweek,* in their 1986 test of a 328GTS still complained that tall drivers ended up looking through the heavily-tinted top part of the windscreen, or, with the top in place, brushed their head on the ceiling. And they found the pedals too close together: "When driving the car for the first time, it takes real concentration to avoid hitting more than one pedal at once," they warned.

Overall, in terms of creature comfort, the 308 was never anything one could brag about and

In the 328, the console switches were up-dated from the 308's toggles to twist knobs or rockers. But the gated shifter stayed true to Ferrari tradition.

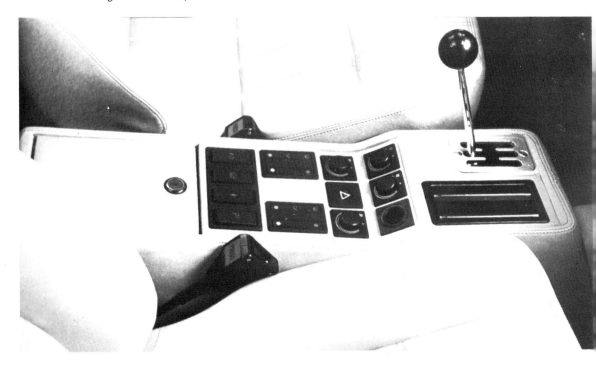

To prevent damage in shipping, 328's are fitted with foam protectors before they leave the plant.

the 328 is only slightly better. But, as **Autoweek** said "Ferrari is not so current; it is falling quickly behind the pack."

The Handling

On paper, mid-engined cars promise the ultimate in handling. That's because they tend to be less nose-heavy (like front wheel drive cars are) or less tail-heavy (like rear-engined cars are). But, in reality, not *all* mid-engined cars have ideal handling.

The reason that the 308 and its successor, the 328, are mid-engined is because, theoretically, such a layout permits a near ideal weight distribution. Thus, it would be possible to have a car with neither understeer or oversteer, but simply "neutral" handling. That's the theory. In practice, the 308 and 328 both have more weight on the rear than on the front. **Road & Track**, in their May 1986 issue quoted the figures as:

1983 308GTSi   42% front/58% rear
1986 328GTS   44% front/56% rear

So much for the theory of mid-engined cars

having equal weight distribution front and rear, for the 1984-'87 Corvette is closer to 50/50 than the 328 and it is a front-engined car!

Unfortunately; **Fast Lane's** testers thought the increased speed makes coping with the chassis more of a struggle at the limit. Even the fat 225-width rear tires can let go and it takes skill to catch it. Said **Fast Lane:** "It's easily caught, but you need to be confident, quick and accurate, lest the yaw swing back the opposite way."

Their opinion was echoed by all the magazines – that the driver who steers the care precisely will be rewarded, while the driver who steers sloppily, or who makes too sudden a transition from gas to brake in a turn, will have problems.

Road & Track's testers worried about the fact that, as you reach the limit of adhesion, the "rear wheel bias takes over and the 328, like many mid-engined cars, becomes an over-steerer." They blamed this partly on the tires, saying that they were "relatively narrow," though Ferrari had fattened up the rear tire size considerably from the first 308 models. **Road & Track** never neared saying that the switch from understeer to oversteer at the limit was

114

dangerous but their warning was there — you can't let a mid-engined car get away from you, or it's going to take some awfully skillful driving to go to opposite lock and recover so you don't fall off the road.

Autoweek, whose road testers had complained about the stiff ride of the 328GTS, praised the handling, saying "You think and that is where you go. The level of grip is so high that there is no way to get close to finding out the limit on public roads." They apparently did not think that the 328 driver would get "out of sorts," saying "you can get the tail out, but the car is so forgiving that the tail just comes back as the revs rise and the surplus power decreases.

Suffice to say that, in ordinary driving situations, the 328 driver will not have to worry about spinning out. But he will have to be more careful about braking in a turn or even lifting his foot off the throttle in a turn than does the driver of a front-engined Ferrari.

In other words, without much effort, the driver of a mid-engined street Ferrari can go around a race course as fast as a front-engined Ferrari. But if the driver of a mid-engined Ferrari gets into trouble, ie. spins out, it is going to take a different set of actions to "catch it" than

he's learned in front engined cars.

In sum...

At this writing, the Ferrari 328 may sti evolve further. The talk is of a 408 version wit a surface re-styling similar to the Testarossa strakes and all, and a 4-liter QV engine. Othe speculation is that a full convertible versio will be available in imitation of one that a Ge man firm, DP, has been making for years.

The problem is that, if the next new model i still using the same basic car, that th shortcomings will become more apparen compared to the increasing sophistication o other cars on the market. In Europe, it was pos sible in 1987 to buy sedans that would ou accelerate the Ferrari 328 to 150 mph! and i America, the Mustang GT, a lowly $12,000 ca could keep with a 308 up to 140 mph!

But sheer speed capability isn't the onl measure of a car, and *Autoweek* said it best i 1986: "It is hard," they wrote, "to design magi into a car." They felt "in this area, Ferra almost always succeeds. The 328 has the pe formance it needs to sustain the magic, fo now, anyway, for now...."

The 328 side view is little changed from the 308. New is the wrap-around flat black front spoiler, the flush foor handles, a new rear undertray, and slightly re-styled 5-spoke "star" mags.

Instead of separate aftermarket fog lamps as employed previously, the 328 had designed-in fog lamps that only fit the 328, as on the Testarossa.

Although this official Ferrari photo shows two "hard" suitcases in a 328, it would have to be factory-fitted luggage to fit. Otherwise, it's mostly a "soft-baggage" type of car.

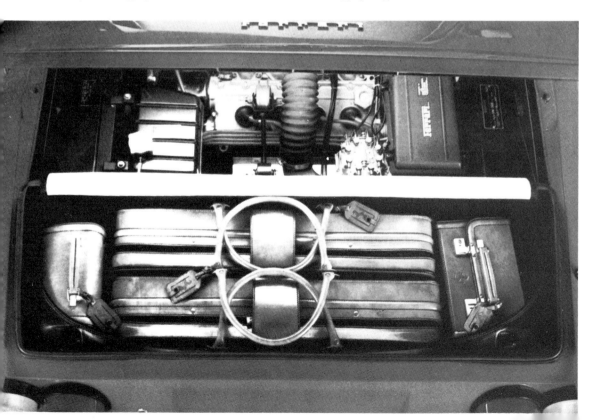

APPENDIX: UPDATES

The GTB/GTS series has gone through only minor variations since its inception in 1976. Here are some of the year-by-year up-dates.

	Model	Comments
1976	GTB only	Leather upholstery. Michelin XWX only. Fiberglass body–1st 200 cars. Dry sump (Europe std.) Thermal Reactor. Support rod supporting engine lid
1977	GTB only	All the above plus: Steel body replacing fiberglass
1978	GTB & GTS	Most of the above plus: One air pump and 3-way catalytic converters on U.S. models. Deep spoiler optional in Europe. 285bhp engine optional in Europe. P7's available in Europe on "16" wheels. Wet sump only on GTS models. Support rod supporting engine lid.
1979	GTB & GTS	Most of the above plus: Gas struts supporting engine lid.
1980	GTB & GTS	New upholstery design. Clock & oil temp. gauge moved to console. Loose weave ceiling replaced vinyl. Mid '80: Michelin TRX radials & new wheel stds. Carpeted scuff panels with open-top door pockets. Fuel injection std. Clutch and gearchange linkage changed to lighten effort.
1981	GTB & GTS	Re-arrange clock & oil temp to horizontal on console. 2 tone Boxer bottom optional.
1982	GTB & GTS	208 Turbo announced in Europe with cloth upholstery, boost gauge on console, digital clock, vented hood, NACA ducts, roof spoiler. Change to aluminum "star" mags on all V8 models. Pressurized gearbox installed on GTB/GTS

TECHNICAL SPECIFICATION

GTB/GTS U.S. version [European version]

Engine

Type	4-Stroke petrol water-cooled
Configuration	V8 cylinder inclined 90°
Bore	81 mm 3.19 cu.in.
Stroke	71 mm 2.79 cu in.
Capacity	2926.9 cu cm 178.62 cu. in.
Compression ratio	8.8:1
Horsepower	214 for fuel injected version at 6600 rpm
	240 at 6600 rpm
	[255 at 6600 rpm]

Cylinder Block

Description	Silalumin casting with axis of cylinder bores inclined 46° from vertical when viewed from flywheel end
Crankshaft	Steel forging with integral balance weights. Five main bearings.

Cylinder Head

	Silalumin alloy, hemi-shaped combustion chambers
Valves	Overhead with direct operation through inverted bucket type tappets
Camshaft	4 overhead camshafts driven by cogged belt from crankshaft centerwheel

Lubrication

Type	Wet sump (except for 1976–77 GTB coupe and all European coupes to 1977 both fiberglass and metal bodies)

Ignition

Distributor	Dual Marelli with contact breaker points* [Single Marelli with contact breaker points] driven off forward bank
Coil	18.5.

Fuel System

Petrol tank capacity	16.3 Imp. gal. 21.1 U.S. gal. 74 liters.
Carburetors	Four Weber 40 DCNF (1980 on: Bosch K–Jetronic fuel injection)
Choke	Manual
Air filter	Combined air cleaner and silencer with replaceable element.
Exhaust	Iron/aluminum four branch manifold, catalytic converters, air pump
Fuel pump	Electric

Electrical Equipment

Battery	Negative earth 12 volt
Capacity	66 amps
	770-watt alternator

* With "i" version, single Marelli-Digiplex without breaker points and static advance

Cooling System	Pressurized "No Loss" cooling system comprising a sealed radiator mounted in front and a metal expansion tank in the rear.
Pump	Impeller pump
Fan	Two aluminum fans with viscous coupling. Electrically-driven. Thermostatically-controlled.
Exhaust System	Twin mild steel down pipes from the manifold running into a transverse silencer with outlet into twin sets of tailpipes.

Transmission

Gearbox	Five speed all synchromesh with gate-type selector
Clutch	Diaphragm clutch with single dry plate hydraulically-operated

Ratios, gearbox	1st	2nd	3rd	4th	Top	Reverse
	3.59	2.35	1.69	1.24	0.95	3.24
Overall	13.32	8.719	6.274	4.611	3.529	12.036

Rear axle	Independent rear suspension with constant velocity joints at transaxle coupling. Limited-slip differential.
Final drive ratio	3.71:1 [4.06]
Roads speeds per 1000 rpm: in top gear	27.73 mph [19.3 mph]

Suspension

Front	Independent. Telescopic shock absorbers and co-axial coil springs.
Rear	Independent. Upper and lower A-arms. Coil springs. Telescopic hydraulic damper units. Anti-roll bar.

Wheels and Tyres

Wheels-type	Die-cast alloy wheels with flat rims. Five stud fixing. TRX wheels: 15½" × 7½". Normal 14" × 6½" (14" × 7½" in US)
Tyres-type	Tubeless radial ply
Size	205/70VR14 XWX (220/55VR 390 with "i" version)
Pressures	30/34

Brakes	Hydraulically-operated divided system by tandem master cylinders with front and rear discs. Mechanical hand-brake operating on rear brakes.
Front Discs Diameter	10.7"
Rear Discs Diameter	10.9"

Steering

Type	Rack and pinion
Wheel	Three-spoked dished steering wheel with padded rim.
Diameter	14"
Turns, lock-to-lock	3.3
Turning circle	39.3

Body	Two door four seater steel body* of unitized construction built atop a tubular frame. Alloy front & rear deck lids. Safety bumpers front & rear.

Interior

Seating	Two individual reclining front seats with adjustable head restraints.

*1976 only – Fiberglass body

Upholstery	Leather or leather and cloth trim. Moulded pile carpeting with driver's heel pad.
Seat belts	Inertia-reel harnesses used front and rear.
Interior equipment	Dipping rear view mirror. Passed sun visors. Cigar lighter. Clock. Interior light operated by door switches.

Electrical Equipment

Instruments and warning lights	Set into fascia panel in front of the driver. Speedometer containing total mileage odometer. Tachometer 0–10,000 rpm. RED Line 7700 rpm.
Warning lights	Brake failure. Parking brake. Alternator. Low Fuel. Fan on. Rear window heat. Lights on. Hazard. High-beam. Directionals.
Controls and switches	Fascia-mounted heater and air conditioner controls. L. H. Drive stalk controls direction indicators. Fascia-mounted toggles for fog lamps, warning flashers, defroster fan.
Horn	Twin Fiamm electrically actuated
Windscreen wipers	Twin electrically-operated self-parking rack driver windscreen wipers, black anti-glare finish. Electric pump-operated washer with plastic reservoir in engine compartment.

Lighting

Headlamps	Twin 5″ diameter retractable headlamps on each side, sealed-beam in U.S.
Side lamps	Side lamps housed in front fenders
Rear lamps	Rear light cluster in rear valance panel with stop/tail lamps, reflectors, direction indicators and reversing lamps.

Heating and Ventilation

A heater/demister unit mounted in the dash panel incorporating a water-heated element delivers fresh air of required temperature to the interior and the windscreen. Variable direction outlets are located in the center of the fascia. Three-speed booster fan.

Acceleration through the gears	U.S.	Secs ("i" version)	European
0–30 mph	2.5	2.5	2.5
0–40 mph	3.7	3.8	3.4
0–50 mph	5.5	5.3	5.0
0–60 mph	7.2	7.4	6.6
0–70 mph	9.6	10.1	8.6
0–80 mph	12.2	na	10.6
Standing ¼-mile	15.8	15.8	15.0
Maximum speed	139 mph	na	154 mph

TECHNICAL SPECIFICATION

Mondial 8 U.S. version [European version]

Engine

Type	4-Stroke petrol water-cooled	
Configuration	V8 cylinder inclined 90°	
Bore	81 mm	3.19 cu. in
Stroke	71 mm	2.79 cu. in.
Capacity	2926.9 cu cm	178.62 cu.in.
Compression ratio	8.1:1	[8.8:1]
Horsepower	205 bhp at 6600 rpm	
	[214 bhp at 6600 rpm]	

Cylinder Block

Description — Silalumin casting with axis of cylinder bores inclined 46° from vertical when viewed from flywheel end.

Crankshaft — Steel forging with integral balance weights. Five main bearings.

Cylinder Head — Silalumin alloy, hemi-shaped combustion chambers

Valves — Overhead with direct operation through inverted bucket type tappets

Camshaft — 4 overhead camshafts driven by cogged belt from crankshaft centerwheel

Lubrication

Type — Wet sump

Ignition

Distributor — Single Marelli Breakerless electronic

Fuel System

Petrol tank capacity — 17.6 Imp gal. 122.2 US gal. 84 liters

Carburetors — Bosch K-Jetronic fuel injection

Choke — Manual

Air filter — Combined air cleaner and silencer with replaceable element

Exhaust — Iron/aluminum four branch manifold, dual 3-way catalytic convertors, air injection, exhaust gas recirculation

Fuel pump — Electric

Electrical Equipment

Battery — Negative earth 12 volt

Capacity — 66 amps
900 watt alternator

Cooling System — Pressurized "No Loss" cooling system comprising a sealed radiator mounted in front and a metal expansion tank in the rear.

Pump — Impeller pump

Fan — Electrically-driven fan with viscous coupling. Thermostatically-controlled.

Exhaust System

Twin mild steel down pipes from the manifold running into a transverse silencer with outlet into twin sets of tailpipes.

Transmission

Gearbox

Five speed all synchromesh with gate-type selector

Clutch

Diaphragm clutch with single dry plate hydraulically-operated.

Ratios, gearbox

	1st	2nd	3rd	4th	Top	Reverse
	3.419	2.353	1.693	1.244	0.919	3.248
Overall	13.888	9.559	6.878	5.055	3.736	13.194

Rear axle

Independent rear suspension with constant velocity joints at transaxle coupling. Limited-slip differential.

Final drive ratio

3.71:1 [4.063:1]

Road speeds per 1000 rpm in top gear

20.7 mph [20:1 mph]

Suspension

Front

Unequal-length A-arms. Telescopic shock absorbers. Anti-roll bar. Coil springs.

Rear

Independent. Unequal-length A-arms. Coil springs. Telescopic shock absorbers. Anti-roll bar.

Wheels and Tyres

Wheels-type

Die-cast alloy wheels with flat rims. Five stud fixing.

Tyres-type

Tubeless radial ply

Size

240/55 VR–390 TRX

Pressures

30/34

Brakes

Hydraulically-operated divided system by tandem master cylinders with front and rear discs. Mechanical handbrake operating on rear brakes.

Front Discs Diameter

282 mm

Rear Discs Diameter

297 mm

Total Swept Area

2736 sq cm/424 sq. in.

Steering

Type

Rack and pinion

Wheel

Three-spoked dished steering wheel with padded rim.

Turns, lock-to-lock

3.45

Turning circle

41ft

Body

Two door four seater steel body of unitized construction built atop a tubular frame. Alloy front and rear deck lids. Safety bumpers front and rear.

Interior

Seating

Two individual reclining front seats with adjustable head restraints.

Upholstery

Leather or leather and cloth trim. Moulded pile carpeting with driver's heel pad.

Seat belts

Inertia-reel harnesses used front and rear.

Interior equipment

Dipping rear view mirror. Passed sun visors. Cigar lighter. Clock. Interior light operated by door switches.

Electrical Equipment

Instruments and warning lights

Set into fascia panel in front of the driver. Speedometer containing total mileage odometer. Tachometer 0–10,000 rpm, RED line 7700 rpm.

Warning lights	Oil pressure, alternator, brake system, hand brake, converter overheat, rear window heater, choke, seatbelts, hazard, parking lights, low beam, high beam, cornering lights, directionals, check panel
Controls and switches	Fascia-mounted heater and air conditioner controls. L.H. Drive stalk controls direction indicators. Fascia-mounted toggles for fog lamps, warning flashers, defroster fan.
Horn	Twin Fiamm electrically actuated
Windscreen wipers	Twin electrically-operated self-parking rack driver windscreen wipers, black anti-glare finish. Electric pump-operated washer with plastic reservoir in engine compartment.

Lighting

Headlamps	Twin 5″ diameter retractable headlamps on each side, sealed-beam in U.S.
Side lamps	Side lamps housed in front fenders
Rear lamps	Rear light cluster in rear valence panel with stop/tail lamps, reflectors, direction indicators and reversing lamps.

Heating and Ventilation

A heater/demister unit mounted in the dash panel incorporating a water-heated element delivers fresh air of required temperature to the interior and the windscreen. Variable direction outlets are located in the center of the fascia. Three-speed booster fan.

Acceleration through the gears	Secs
0–30 mph	2.92
0–40 mph	4.11
0–50 mph	6.66
0–60 mph	8.80
0–70 mph	11.07
0–80 mph	15.00
0–100 mph	28.1
Standing ¼ mile	16.29 secs.
Maximum speed	139 mph